egyptian religion

egyptian religion

the beliefs of ancient egypt explored and explained

lucia gahlin

southwater

For Richard and Dexter

This edition is published by Southwater

Southwater is an imprint of
Anness Publishing Ltd
Hermes House, 88–89 Blackfriars Road
London SE1 8HA
tel. 020 7401 2077; fax 020 7633 9499
info@anness.com

© Anness Publishing Ltd 2002

Published in the USA by Southwater
Anness Publishing Inc.
fax 212 807 6813

Distributed in the UK by
The Manning Partnership
tel. 01225 852 727; fax 01225 852 852

Distributed in the USA by
National Book Network
tel. 301 459 3366; fax 301 459 1705

Distributed in Canada by
General Publishing
tel. 416 445 3333; fax 416 445 5991

Distributed in Australia by
Pan Macmillan Australia
tel. 1300 135 113; fax 1300 135 103

Distributed in New Zealand by
The Five Mile Press (NZ) Ltd
tel. (09) 444 4144; fax (09) 444 4518

A CIP catalogue record for this book is
available from the British Library.

Publisher: Joanna Lorenz
Managing Editor: Helen Sudell
Project Editor: Jennifer Schofield
Designer: Jez McBean
Illustrator: Stuart Carter
Production Controller: Joanna King

Previously published as part of a larger
compendium, *Egypt: Gods, Myths and Religion*

1 2 3 4 5 6 7 8 9 10

CONTENTS

MEDITERRANEAN SEA

● Tanis

the pyramids at Giza are
one of the wonders of the
ancient world

QATARA DEPRESSION

FAIYUM

SINAI

the earliest step pyramid
was built at Saqqara for
the pharaoh Djoser

● Giza
● Abusir
● Saqqara
● Dahshur
Lisht ●
Meidum ●

● Lahun/Kahun
● Hawara

**OASIS OF
BAHRIA**

the bent pyramid
at Dahshur

WESTERN LIBYAN DESERT

● Beni Hasan

● el-Bershaer

● Tell el-Amarna

EASTERN DESERT

the pyramid at Meidum
built around the middle of
the third millennium BC

● el-Badari

**FARAFRA
OASIS**

Abydos ●

the Valley of the Kings
houses the tombs of 62
kings and nobles, including
king Tutankhamun

● Naqada
● Thebes
● Valley of the Kings/
Deir el-Medina
● Gebelein

**DAKHLA
OASIS**

Hierakonopolis ●

**KHARGA
OASIS**

● Burial Sites Mentioned in Text

1ST CATARACT ←

Burial Sites

The pyramids of Egypt are one of the seven wonders of the ancient world. Each was built as a mortuary – the eternal resting place of a monarch. Such magnificent monuments stand testament to the unwavering belief of the ancient peoples in a life after death. Later kings were buried below ground in tombs no less grand, which were cut into the surface of rock faces. These mortuaries, like the pyramids, housed precious treasures as well as everyday items that would help the monarch assume his rightful role in the Afterlife.

Yet only the very wealthy could afford grand funerals, and mummification did not exist for the masses. For the ordinary people, a burial alongside the Nile river would ensure that they obtained a place in the Afterlife. Here they would assume a more prosperous and bountiful lifestyle than that which they held on earth.

NORTH

RED SEA

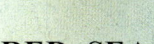

PALESTINE

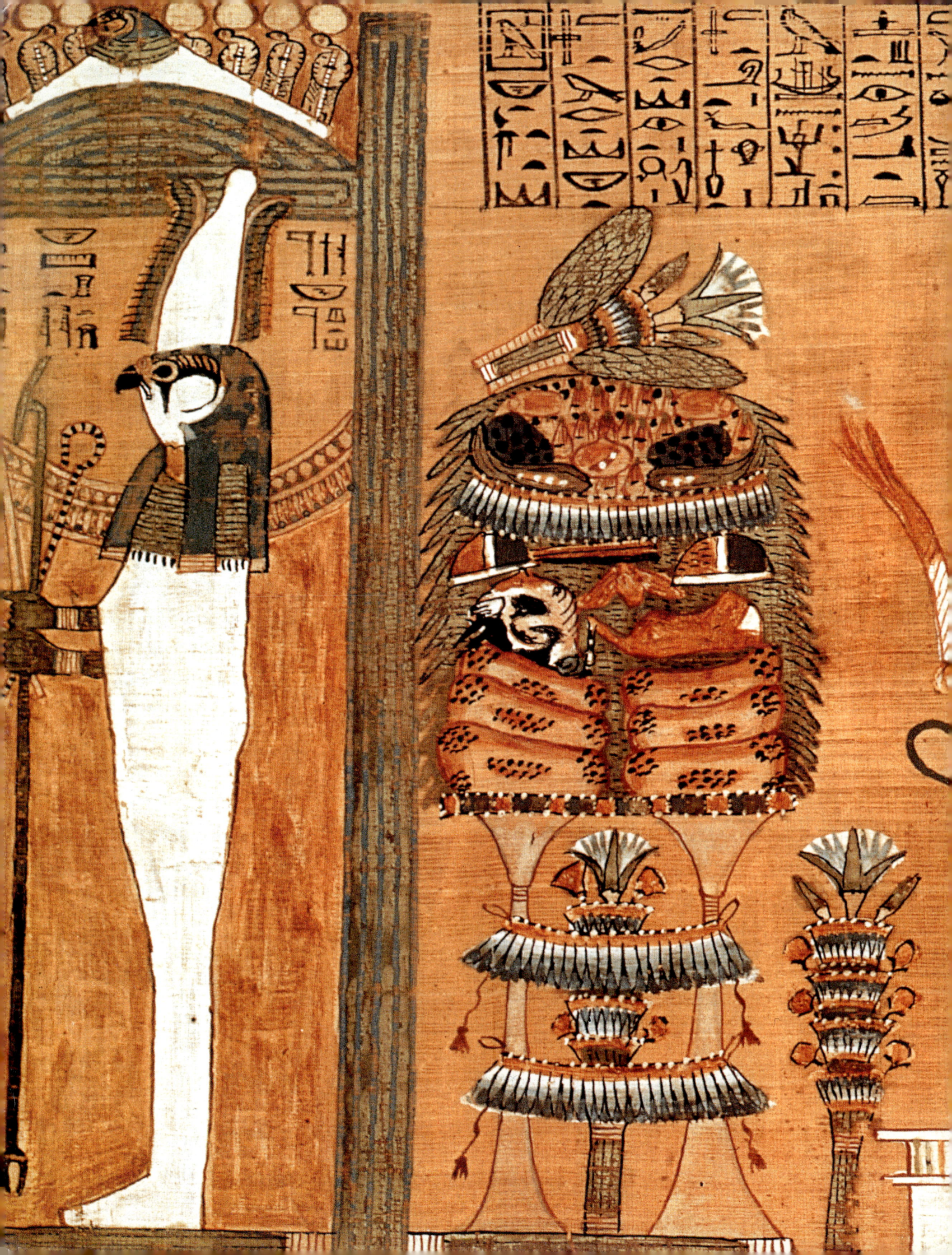

Funerary Religion

The ancient Egyptians clearly believed in an Afterlife long before the advent of writing and a formalized state religion. Burials dating from the Predynastic Period (c.5500–c.3100 BC) contain a range of objects of daily use, such as storage jars, flint knives, ivory combs and slate palettes. Their presence suggests the belief that such 'funerary equipment' was required for the Afterlife.

These excavated burials reveal that the bodies were buried in shallow oval graves at the edge of the desert. The hot dry sand rapidly absorbed moisture, so that bacteria could not breed and cause decay. The body in the British Museum, London, now known as 'Ginger', was buried in the sand at Gebelein in c.3200 BC, and survived intact for more than 5,000 years.

With the emergence of a social élite demanding grander burials, bodies began to be buried in coffins and underground chambers lined with wood, mudbrick or even stone, and they quickly began to rot. Mummification was developed and continued in use until the rise of Christianity in the early fourth century AD. But an elaborate burial was a luxury – although a belief in the Afterlife was no doubt universal, the people of Egypt were equipped for it to varying degrees.

◀ *From the New Kingdom (c.1550–c.1069 BC) it was customary for wealthy Egyptians to include a papyrus roll inscribed with spells and vignettes from the Book of the Dead in their tombs.*

Beliefs About the Afterlife

The preparations that accompanied burials from as early as Predynastic times (c.5500–c.3100 BC) reveal that the ancient Egyptians must have had beliefs about the existence of an Afterlife from very early on. These ideas were certainly formed well before the emergence of Pharaonic Egypt as we know it; that is, before the country was unified into an influential state with a sole ruler and an efficient, centralized government. Pre-dating any evidence for social stratification and the existence of a wealthy minority, there is evidence for burials involving the deposit of funerary goods in the grave alongside the body.

These items were not elaborate or specially crafted ceremonial artefacts, but basic objects of daily life, such as pots, tools and weapons. Presumably the people buried with these things believed that they would need them in a practical way after death. After all, a simple pot is unlikely to have been a token of sentiment or a prized possession; its presence in a tomb must have been considered functional.

▼ An Egyptian lady would have been buried with a selection of objects intended to ensure that she would be able to eat, adorn herself with jewellery, cosmetics and perfumed unguents, and perform rituals in the Afterlife. New Kingdom.

▲ In a land of extreme heat and vast desert expanses, a pool and the cool shade of a date palm were heavenly. By depicting them on the wall of his tomb, Pashedu hoped to enjoy their benefits in the Afterlife. 19th Dynasty. Thebes.

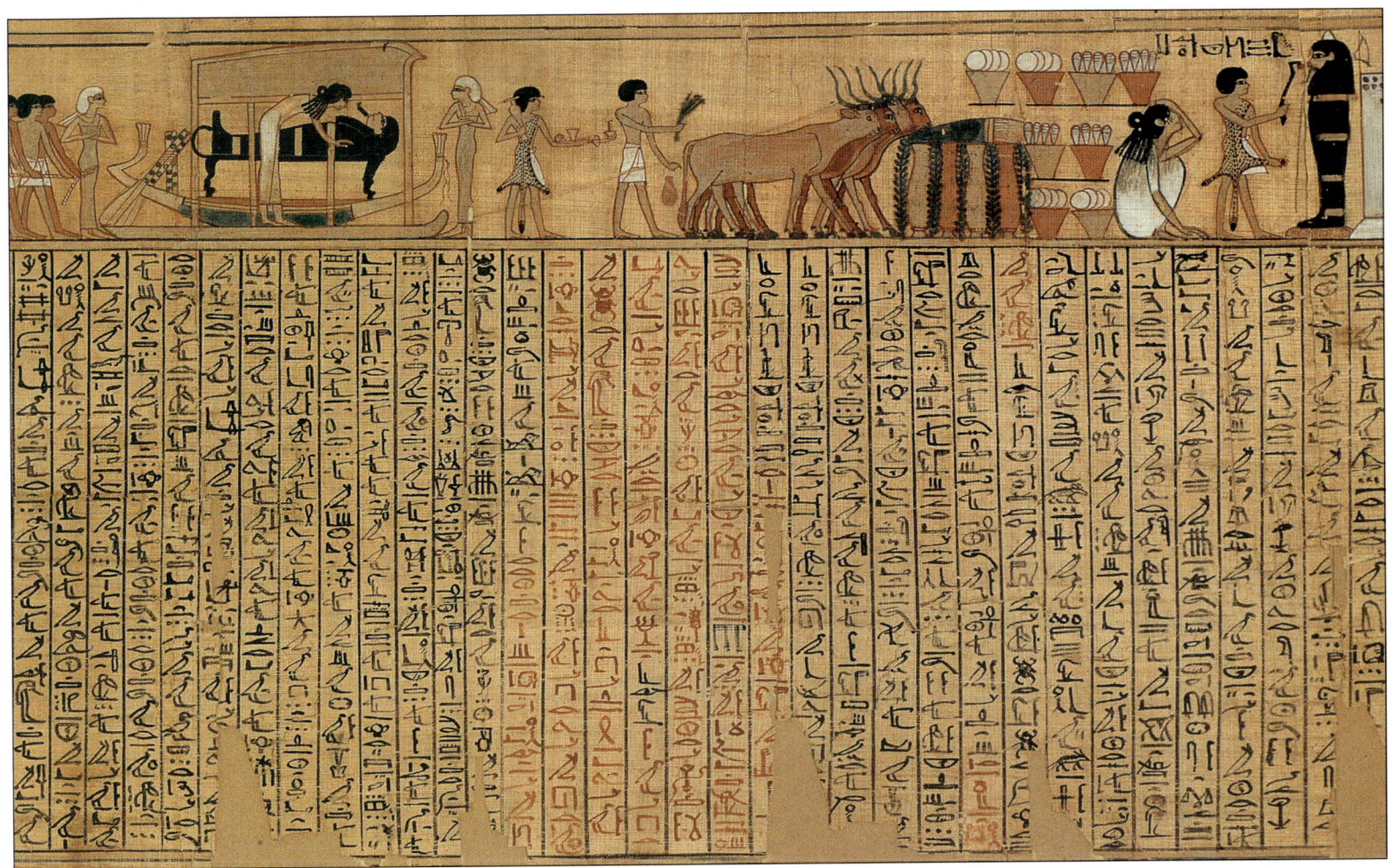

Journeying into the Afterlife

The predynastic custom of burying dead bodies in the foetal position may suggest a belief in the concept of rebirth. Also, the accidental or deliberate unearthing of perfectly preserved bodies may have led the early Egyptians to believe that the dead were living on in some way. The emergence of the practice of mummification early in the Dynastic Period reveals the strongly held belief that the body was required to be intact for the Afterlife.

We can have no idea of what the ancient Egyptians imagined the Afterlife to be until they were able to write down a description of it. The funerary texts that were buried with the dead tell us that they ascended to the Afterlife and that it was located in the heavens – the realm of the sun. Several methods of ascent appear to have been possible. These included riding on the back of a falcon, goose or other bird; being wafted upwards with burning incense; climbing up a ladder formed by the outstretched arms of the gods; or travelling on a reed float or barque that was sailed, rowed or towed. The journey into the Afterlife was no mean feat – all manner of demons and other hazardous obstacles had to be bypassed and overcome. The funerary texts provided guidelines and directions for the routes to be taken, and certain spells and recitations to be uttered at the appropriate time.

Domains of the dead

The ancient Egyptians imagined the Afterlife as a perfect version of life as they knew it in the Nile Valley, with a constant superabundance of produce. The vignettes on papyrus that accompany the text in the Book of the Dead, and the scenes painted on the walls of non-royal tombs, also provide us with a picture of the Afterlife. They tend to show the tomb owner and his wife toiling in the fields, which they did not for one moment expect actually to do (or at least they hoped not to). They certainly would have taken precautions to safeguard against the possibility of any hard work (see *Shabtis*).

▲ *The Book of the Dead includes illustrations of the final procession of the mummified body to the tomb and the last rites before burial, such as the Opening of the Mouth ceremony. The chain of events is depicted here on the papyrus of the high official Nebqed. New Kingdom.*

Egyptian paradise

The Egyptian paradise was called the Field of *Hetep* ('satisfaction' or 'offerings') – the land of Osiris, the god of the dead. The Coffin Texts (spells 464–468) and Chapter 110 of the Book of the Dead describe this land. It was associated with the western horizon (the place of the setting sun) and was imagined as a luscious place. Its fields were irrigated by channels full of water; its crops of emmer wheat, barley and flax grew tall and strong; its fruit trees were heavy with their loads of ripe dates and figs.

▶ *Sennedjem is depicted standing at the gate of the other world. A similar illustration was used to represent the vertical tomb shaft that separated the tomb chapel from the subterranean burial chamber below. 19th Dynasty. Thebes.*

The iconography of the ancient Egyptian religious belief system was strongly influenced by an underlying concept of duality – the importance of opposite but interdependent entities. The two horizons occurred frequently in both the solar and funerary aspects of the religion. Coupled with the Field of *Hetep*, which was associated with the western horizon, was the Field of *Iaru* ('reeds'), a place of purification that was associated with the eastern horizon, the site of the purification and 'rebirth' of the sun each dawn. Two other names that crop up in the funerary texts are '*Duat*' and '*Imhet*'. They were identified as separate locations in the sky: *Duat* referred to the eastern horizon, and *Imhet* to the western one. These terms might best be translated as 'Afterworld'. They are often rendered as 'Underworld' or 'Netherworld', but these translations can be misleading because the deceased appears to have ascended to them. Another name that came to be used as a general term for the Afterworld was *Rosetau* (literally, 'passage of dragging'). It originally referred to the sloping entranceway of a tomb; it was later used as the name for the necropolis of Memphis, and afterwards of Abydos.

Coming closer to the gods

The ancient Egyptians used strong visual images to illustrate, and even animate, their beliefs. The Afterworld was divinely personified as Aker. This was an earth divinity represented as a narrow tract of land with a human or lion head at each end, or sometimes in the form of two lions seated back to back, one facing east and one west (sometimes with the symbol for the horizon between them). These two creatures were thought to guard the entrance and exit to the Afterworld.

There is also evidence that the ancient Egyptians had a concept of an 'undersky' (*Nenet*) and an underworld where demons lived upside-down. As a result, because their mouths were where their anuses should have been, they had to eat their own faeces. Luckily, spells existed to avoid having to face what this place had to offer.

By dying and passing into the Afterlife, an individual was thought to become closer to the gods, and perhaps even influence the divine world. There is evidence to show that the dead were believed to possess supernatural powers that could solve various problems for the living. However, as well as proving helpful, the dead could cause serious disturbances for the living. The unsettled dead were often blamed for causing all kinds of distress, including illness. ◆

Ka, Ba and *Akh*

There are three important words which crop up repeatedly in the ancient Egyptian funerary texts, and which are variously translated as 'spirit' and 'soul'. It is probably best to leave them untranslated, because it is very difficult to be sure exactly what these terms meant to the ancient Egyptians, and a word such as 'soul' has connotations that would have been unfamiliar to them.

The hieroglyph used to write *ka* was a pair of arms, but in art the *ka* was represented as an individual's slightly smaller double. For example, in the 'divine birth' scenes on the walls of Hatshepsut's mortuary temple at Deir el-Bahri, two small and identical figures are depicted on a potter's wheel. These are the Eighteenth-Dynasty ruler Hatshepsut (c.1473–c.1458 BC) and her *ka* being created by the ram-headed creator god Khnum.

The *ka* was thought to come into being at the birth of an individual. Dying was sometimes described as 'joining one's *ka*'. The *ka* was intimately linked with the physical body, which was regarded

▼ *The* ba-*bird not only represented the concept of the 'soul', but also anonymous gods or powers, and as such was present on the walls of New Kingdom royal tombs.*

as the vessel for the *ka* after death. This explains the belief in the need for the survival of the body, and the measures taken to preserve it whenever possible. *Ka* is often translated as 'spirit' or 'vital force', as in the creative life force of an individual that enabled the generations to continue through the ages. It was believed that the *ka* required food and drink, so offerings were made to it for as long as possible after death. In fact the word *ka* sometimes means 'sustenance', depending on the context.

The hieroglyph used to write *ba* was a Jabiru stork, while in funerary art it was represented as a bird with a human head, and sometimes with human arms. The ancient Egyptian idea of the *ba* appears to have been similar to our concept of personality, that is the non-physical attributes that make any human being unique. It is possible that it also implied the moral essence of a person's motivation and movement. It was considered more mobile than the *ka* and it enabled the dead person to move about in the Afterlife. The ancient Egyptian word for 'ram' was also *ba*, and it was probably for this reason that the ram-headed deity Khnum was regarded as the *ba* of Re, the sun god.

The hieroglyph used to write *akh* was a crested ibis, although it was often portrayed as a *shabti*-like mummiform figure (see *Shabtis*). It may well have been considered the result of the successful reunion at death of the *ba* and the *ka*, and it is sometimes translated as 'transfigured spirit'. Those who failed to achieve this transfiguration were condemned to eternal death.

Together with the *ka, ba,* and *akh*, two other important elements of a person's being, in both life and death, were their name and their shadow. It was believed vital to ensure that these two elements were remembered and protected after death in order that the deceased should survive in the Afterlife. ◆

▲ *Funerary statues were seen as images of the* ka *of the dead, and might incorporate the* ka *symbol on their head, as in the case of this statue of Awibre Hor.*

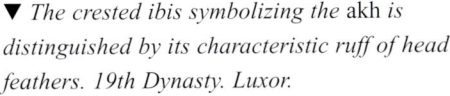

▼ *The crested ibis symbolizing the* akh *is distinguished by its characteristic ruff of head feathers. 19th Dynasty. Luxor.*

The Weighing of the Heart

The ancient Egyptians believed that, when they died, they would be judged on their behaviour during their lifetime before they could be granted a place in the Afterlife. This judgment ceremony was called the Weighing of the Heart, and was recorded in Chapter 125 of the funerary text known as the Book of the Dead. For this reason it is most commonly recorded and illustrated on papyrus.

The ceremony was believed to take place before Osiris, the chief god of the dead and the Afterlife, and a tribunal of 42 deities. Standing before the tribunal, the deceased was asked to name each of the divine judges and swear that he or she had not committed any of a long list of possible offences, ranging from raising the voice to stealing. This was the 'negative confession'. If found innocent, the deceased was declared 'true of voice' and was allowed to proceed into the Afterlife. The proceedings were recorded by Thoth, the scribe of the gods, and the deity of wisdom and the scribal profession. He was often depicted with an ibis head, writing on a roll of papyrus. His other animal form – the baboon – was sometimes depicted sitting on the pivot of the scales of justice.

Gobbling the heart

The symbolic ritual that accompanied this trial was the weighing of the heart of the deceased on a pair of enormous scales. It was weighed against the principle of truth and justice (*maat*), represented by a feather, the symbol of the goddess of truth, order and justice, Maat. If the heart balanced against the feather then the deceased would be granted a place in the Fields of *Hetep* and *Iaru* (see *Beliefs about the Afterlife*). If it was heavy with the weight of wrongdoings, the balance would sink, and the heart would be grabbed and devoured by a terrifying beast that sat ready and waiting by the scales. This beast was Ammit ('the gobbler'), a composite animal with the head of a crocodile, the front legs and body of a lion or leopard, and the back legs of a hippopotamus.

Ensuring success

The ancient Egyptians considered the heart to be the centre of thought, memory and emotion. It was thus associated with intellect and personality and was considered the most important organ in the body. It was deemed to be essential for rebirth into the Afterlife. Unlike the other internal organs, it was never removed and embalmed separately, because its presence in the body was crucial.

If the deceased was found to have done wrong and the heart weighed down

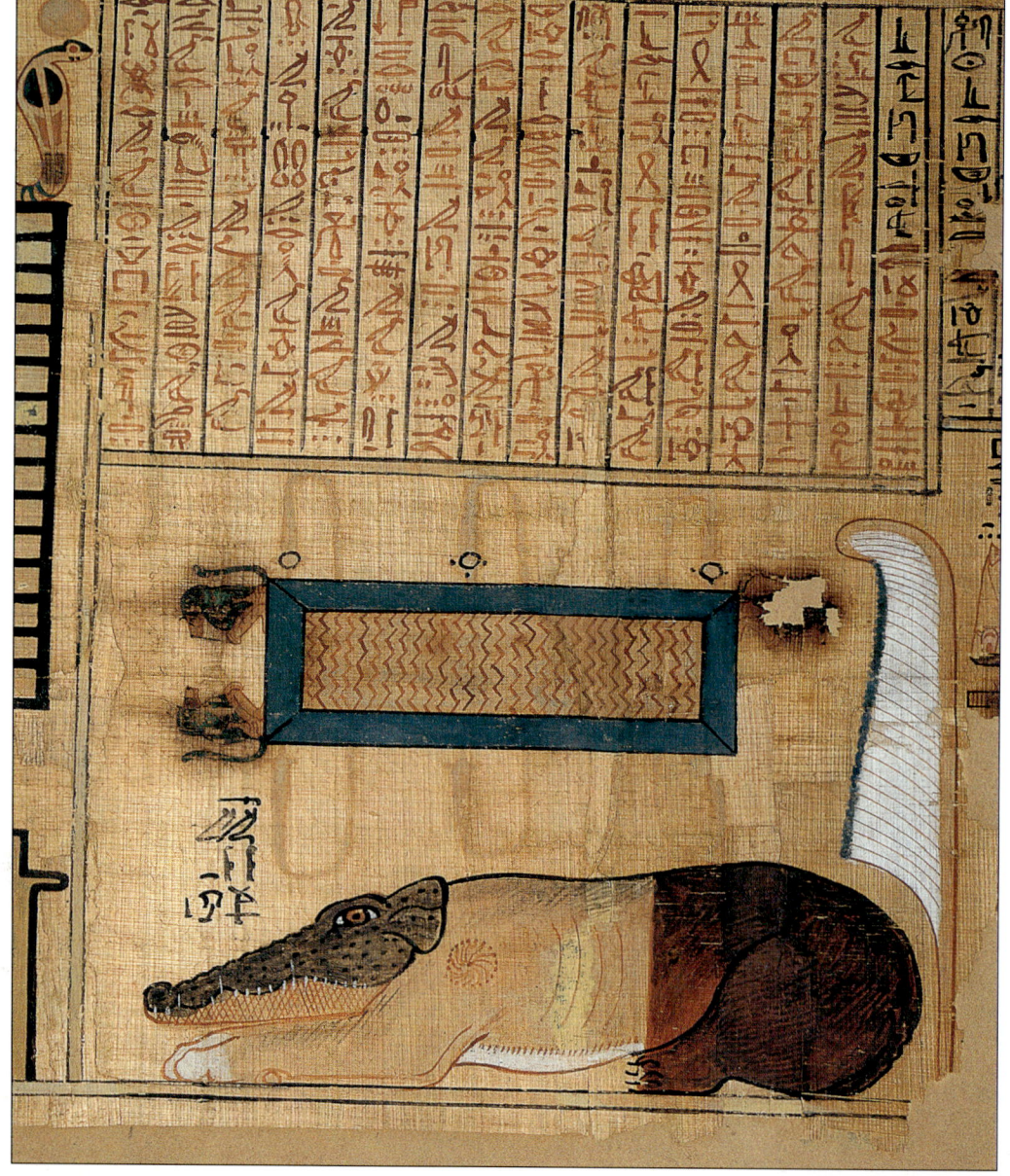

◀ *The Book of the Dead of Nebqed includes one of the earliest depictions of the composite beast Ammit, part crocodile, part lion and part hippopotamus. 18th Dynasty.*

▲ *The Weighing of the Heart took place in the Hall of Double Maat. In this scene from the Book of the Dead of Hunefer a lotus flower grows out of a pool beneath Osiris's throne, and on it stand the Four Sons of Horus.*

the scales, he or she was not thought to enter a place of torment like hell, but to cease to exist at all. This idea would have terrified the ancient Egyptians. However, for those who could afford to include Chapter 125 of the Book of the

▼ *'Heart scarabs' were important protective amulets placed on the mummy to prevent the heart from bearing witness against the deceased. New Kingdom.*

Dead in their tombs, it was almost guaranteed that they would pass successfully into the Afterlife. This is because the ancient Egyptians believed in the magical qualities of the actual writings and illustrations in funerary texts. By depicting the heart balancing in the scales against the feather of Maat (sometimes with the aid of a little adjusting on the part of Anubis, the jackal-headed god of cemeteries and embalming), they ensured that would be the favourable outcome. The entire ceremony was, after all, symbolic.

Following the Weighing of the Heart, the organ was returned to its owner. To make quite sure that this did happen, Chapters 26–29 of the Book of the Dead were spells to ensure that the heart was returned and that it could never be removed again. ◆

Heart scarabs

Those ancient Egyptians who could afford the luxury of extensive funerary equipment took every precaution possible to ensure their survival through the judgment ceremony. A particularly useful addition to the burial would have been a large 'heart scarab' wrapped up in the bandaging (see *Funerary Amulets*). This form of protection was invented at least as early as the Thirteenth Dynasty and, according to the Book of the Dead, should be made of a specific green stone (*nemehef*), which has not been identified with certainty.

The scarab was inscribed on the underside with Chapter 30 of the Book of the Dead, a short text which was thought to prevent the heart from owning up to any crimes the person had committed in life:

O my heart which I had upon earth...do not speak against me concerning what I have done...

Mummification

The ancient Egyptians mummified the dead bodies of those who could afford such an elaborate and costly procedure. It is important to remember that this was a practice followed only by the royal family and the wealthier classes of Egyptian society. The word used to describe an embalmed and wrapped body is of course 'mummy', but this is in fact a misnomer because it comes from the Arabic *mummiya*, meaning pitch or bitumen, neither of which were actually used in Egyptian mummification. However, bodies mummified during the Late

▼ *The standing lion was a symbol of protection and defence, and so embalming tables such as this one painted on the wall of Sennedjem's tomb were carved in this way.*

Period (c.747–332 BC) were often so badly embalmed that they were blackened and brittle, and as they were found to burn well it was assumed that they had been dipped in bitumen.

The Greek writer Herodotus made a slightly erroneous account of the mummification process in c.450 BC, and two damaged papyri have survived from the first century AD outlining the final stages of the process. Unfortunately no embalmer's handbook has survived from the Pharaonic Period. Consequently, our understanding of the procedure, and how it developed, is based mainly on examination of the bodies themselves.

In the Early Dynastic Period (c.3100–c.2686 BC) dead bodies were tightly wrapped in strips of resin-soaked linen.

This did not prove to be wholly successful, because although the bandages hardened in the form of the body, the body itself decayed, so during the Third Dynasty (c.2686–c.2613 BC) methods of preserving the body itself were explored. The ancient Egyptians came to realize that if they wanted the body to survive they had to dehydrate it from the inside and the outside at the same time, and that to do this effectively they had to remove the internal organs. Up until this time, the dead had been buried in a contracted foetal position, but it was found to be easier to reach the internal organs if the body was stretched out, so the dead came to be buried in this position.

The oldest surviving mummy dates to the late Fifth Dynasty (c.2400 BC), but it is known that the ancient Egyptians were removing the internal organs, and embalming and burying them separately, at least as early as the Fourth Dynasty, because the internal organs of Queen Hetepheres, the mother of the Great Pyramid builder, Khufu (c.2589–c.2566 BC), were found in a canopic chest.

Purifying the body

Once a successful procedure was arrived at, it appears to have been as follows.

The body was taken to a 'place of purification' (*ibu*). This would probably have been located on the west bank of the Nile, the bank associated with the setting sun and thus the place of the dead. It would need to be sited close to the river for easy access to a good water supply, and undoubtedly as far away as possible from populated sites owing to the nature of its business.

The initial washing of the naked corpse had both a ritual and a practical importance. The body was washed, as was the cult statue in a temple each morning, and as was the sun god Re in the waters of Nun each morning before

being 'reborn' at dawn. The washing was done using a solution of natron, so it would have aided the first stage of preservation. Natron is a salt (a natural compound of sodium carbonate and bicarbonate) that the ancient Egyptians found as crystals along the edges of lakes in the Wadi Natrun, 65km (40 miles) north-west of Cairo. One of the ancient Egyptian names for natron was *neteryt* ('belonging to the god'), presumably because of its use in ritual purification. It was particularly useful in the embalming process because it is a mild antiseptic as well as being an effective dehydrating agent (it absorbs water, thus drying out the body but leaving it flexible).

Preparing the body

The purified body was then removed to the actual place of embalmment (*wabt* or *per nefer*), which was originally an enclosure containing a tent or booth. By the Late Period (c.747–c.332 BC) far more bodies were being embalmed than ever before, so for the first time permanent embalming houses were built of mudbrick. The chief embalmer was known as 'He who Controls the Mysteries' (*hery seshta*), and it is very likely that he would have worn a jackal mask during the rituals accompanying

▲ *This man was not mummified but thanks to his body's direct contact with the hot, dry sand it has survived since c.3200 BC, intact but for the top of one of the forefingers.*

the embalming process in order to imitate the jackal-headed god of embalming, Anubis. His deputy bore the title 'God's Seal-Bearer' (*hetemu netjer*), which had originally been a title held by priests of Osiris, the god of the dead and the Afterlife. According to ancient Egyptian mythology, Osiris had been the first person to be mummified, after his death at the hands of his brother Seth.

Once in the embalming house, the body was stretched out on four wooden blocks on a wooden board (an example of which was found at Thebes). The first priority was to preserve the face, and so the head was probably coated with molten resin. From the Eighteenth Dynasty (c.1550 BC) the brain was removed and discarded, because it was considered to be merely stuffing for the head. Sawdust, resin or resin-soaked linen was pushed inside the skull to ensure that it kept its shape. The ancient Egyptians really had no idea about the function of the brain; they thought that the heart was the seat of thought and emotion in the human body.

▲ *It is uncertain whether depictions of jackal-headed men in the funerary art represent the god Anubis himself, or priests wearing masks in order to represent the deity.*

▲ *Roman encaustic portraits were combined with the Egyptian tradition of mummification in Egypt for about 200 years from the middle of the 1st century AD. In this portrait of Artemidorus he wears a wreath of leaves and berries applied in gold leaf.*

Consequently they never deliberately removed the heart from the body because they believed its presence was crucial at all times and it played a vital part in the judgment of the deceased before he or she was able to pass into the Afterlife.

The major internal organs were removed, but they were embalmed separately and kept safely because the Egyptians believed they were necessary for the continued functioning of the body in the Afterlife. The stomach and intestines were removed through an incision in the lower abdomen (usually on the left side), then the diaphragm was punctured so that the lungs and liver could also be extracted. According to Herodotus and the Sicilian-born historian Diodorus Siculus (c.40 BC), a knife of Ethiopian stone or obsidian was used to make the incision.

Once removed, the internal organs were dried out in crystalline natron, rubbed with sweet-smelling unguents, coated in molten resin and wrapped in linen bandages in four separate packages. These packages were usually then placed in special jars that accompanied the body to the tomb (see *Canopic Jars*), but from the Twenty-first Dynasty (c.1069 BC) they were often placed back in the original positions of the internal organs inside the body. During the Ptolemaic Period (332–30 BC) they were usually placed between the corpse's legs before wrapping.

Embalming

The body, without its internal organs, was packed with temporary stuffing, and covered over with natron for forty days, after which time it would have turned a much darker colour and have become as much as 75% lighter in weight. The temporary stuffing was removed, and the corpse was rinsed out, washed down, dried to prevent mould forming and re-stuffed with wads of linen, linen soaked with resin, bags of natron crystals, sawdust and other materials to help the body keep its shape. During the Late Period (c.747–c.332) bodies were often filled completely with resin.

For both ritual and functional reasons, the body was anointed again, this time with juniper oil, beeswax, natron, spices, milk and wine. The abdominal incision was stitched up, and often covered with gold foil or wax. It was adorned with a protective 'Eye of Horus' – the *udjat* or

▼ *Networks of beads arranged over the entire body of the mummy are typical of the end of the Third Intermediate Period and Saite Era. Images such as winged pectoral scarabs and the Four Sons of Horus were often woven into them. 25th Dynasty.*

wadjat-eye (see *Funerary Amulets*). The nostrils, ears, and mouth were usually plugged with linen, wax, or sometimes onion skins or whole bulbs. Today people use onion to soak up nasty smells, and in folklore it is believed to help combat infection. In ancient Memphis, during the festival of the hawk-headed funerary deity Sokar, his devotees were accustomed to wearing strings of onions. Depending on the wealth and extravagance of the deceased's family, a piece of gold leaf might be placed over the tongue. The whole body was then coated with resin in order to toughen it and make it waterproof.

As well as the practical measures taken, at all times the emphasis was also very much on creating a pleasing appearance to the body. The soles of the feet and palms of the hands might be stained with henna; the cheeks might be rouged; and the lips and the eyebrows might be painted. Sometimes the body was dressed in clothes, sandals and a wig. The bodies of men were often painted with red ochre and that of women with yellow ochre, because these were the standard pigments used to create the skin colour of men and women in art. The bodies of wealthier people were covered in jewellery before the bandaging began. Mummies have been found, dating to the Graeco-Roman Period, with gold leaf on their faces, chests and nails.

Bandaging the body

At last the body was ready for bandaging. This intricate process was carried out by the bandagers (*wetyw*) and took 15 days, beginning with the fingers and toes. It was accompanied by the recitation of magical spells by a Lector Priest (*hery heb*). The bandages

▲ *Anthropoid coffins of the 21st Dynasty often incorporate a pair of crossed red 'braces', over an enlarged collar, in their design. Thebes.*

were linen and were often made out of old clothes, towels, and so on. The most sought-after bandages would have been recycled from the cast-off garments worn by divine statues in the temples and shrines. A vast quantity of linen – up to 375sq m (450sq yd) – was used to wrap one body.

The embalmed body was enveloped in a yellow shroud before being bandaged. Each stage was painted with melted resin. Every attempt was made to ensure that the body looked as perfect as possible so if, for example, a hand was missing, an artificial hand would be inserted into the bandaging. Men were usually wrapped with their arms extended and their hands crossed over their genitals, whereas women's hands were usually placed on their thighs. From the early New Kingdom (c.1550 BC) onwards, kings were wrapped with their arms crossed over their chest, in the manner of Osiris, the god of the Afterlife.

The bandaged body was then inserted into one or more shrouds (usually dyed

red), which were knotted at the top and bottom and held in place by several more bandages. An interesting feature can be found on top of the bandaging (or just below the surface) of mummies dating to the Twenty-first and Twenty-second Dynasties (c.1069–c.715 BC): two red leather straps crossed over the chest, resembling a pair of braces. A peculiarity of many of the mummies dating to the Twenty-fifth Dynasty (c.747–656 BC) and later is a shroud of blue faience beads, very like the Fifth-Dynasty bead net dress from Qau, now in the Petrie Museum of Egyptian Archaeology, London.

Finally, a mummy mask was fitted over the head and shoulders of the body. The mask was usually made of cartonnage – linen or papyrus stiffened with plaster. In the case of royalty it would have been made of gold, and the upper classes sometimes imitated the costliest of masks by having their cartonnage ones gilded. ◆

Funeral preparations

The entire, complicated process of mummification, from the arrival of the corpse at the *ibu*, lasted 70 days. This was the time permitted for the funeral preparation.

It is likely that a period of 70 days was chosen deliberately in connection with the 70 days when the dog star Sirius (divinely personified as the goddess Sopdet) could not be seen because of its alignment with the earth and the sun prior to its heliacal rising. This annual astronomical occurrence heralded the inundation of the Nile and marked the start of the ancient Egyptian New Year (*wep renpet*).

Pyramid Texts

The oldest surviving funerary texts – collections of spells or 'utterances' that accompanied a burial – are those known today as the Pyramid Texts. These were exclusively the prerogative of the king during the Old Kingdom and First Intermediate Period (c.2686–c.2055 BC). They dealt with his protection while he was still alive (particularly against dangerous animals), but were mainly concerned with his death and what was believed to happen to him afterwards. Later versions of funerary texts – known as the Coffin Texts and the Book of the Dead – were not confined to royal burials, and demonstrate the gradual democratization of funerary religion.

Written in hieroglyphs, the earliest appearance of the Pyramid Texts is as inscriptions on the inner walls of the corridors and chambers of the pyramid of Unas (c.2375– c.2345 BC), the last ruler of the Fifth Dynasty. It was built at Saqqara, one of the great cemeteries of the capital city of Memphis. A further eight pyramids of the Sixth Dynasty and early First Intermediate Period (c.2345–c.2125 BC) have been found to contain very similar inscriptions. Five of these pyramids belonged to kings, and the other three to wives of the Sixth-Dynasty ruler Pepi II (c.2278–c.2184 BC). The Pyramid Texts totalled some eight hundred spells, but no one pyramid was inscribed with all of them, the largest collection being the 675 texts found in the pyramid of Pepi II.

The funeral of the king

It has been suggested that the sequence of the spells relates to the funeral of the king, and the procession of his mummified body from the Valley Temple connected with his pyramid to his burial chamber within the pyramid. The king is identified with Osiris, the god of the dead and the Afterlife, and many of the spells in the burial chamber

◄ By the 5th Dynasty the emphasis was no longer on enormous grandeur but on the hieroglyphic inscriptions within pyramids such as that of Teti, and the reliefs on the walls of the associated mortuary temples. Saqqara.

would probably have been recited by the Lector Priest at the funeral. The earliest known recording of the Opening of the Mouth ceremony and early offering rituals are to be found in these texts. The purpose of many of the spells was to protect the dead king in the Afterlife. Because the language in which they are written is archaic in places, it is likely that these were in fact very ancient spells, recorded for the first time in the Old Kingdom.

The emphasis on the cult of the sun god in the texts implies that perhaps they were composed by the priests at Heliopolis, the cult centre of Re. This temple and its priesthood had had close associations with the king since at least the Fourth Dynasty. Utterance 264 is one of many spells that refer to the king's ascension to the realm of the sun. It ends:

The Nurse Canal is opened, the Winding Waterway is flooded, the Fields of Reeds are filled with water, so that the king is ferried over on it to that eastern side of the sky, to the place where the gods fashion him, where he is born again new and young.

The idea was that when the king died he went to join the sun god on his journey through the sky by day and the Netherworld by night. This journey was thought to be made by boat, and it was believed that when the sun god reached

◄ The behaviour attributed to Nut of swallowing and giving birth to the sun – depicted here in Ramesses IX's burial chamber – was ultimately an enigma, as indicated by her epithet shetayit, which means 'mysterious one'.

the eastern horizon, just before dawn, he was purified in Nun, the waters of creation. The rising of the sun was identified with the dead king's rebirth.

Rebirth of the king

It has been suggested that names such as the 'Nurse Canal', 'Winding Waterway' and 'Field of Reeds' found in the Pyramid Texts refer to parts of the sky goddess Nut's anatomy. One mythological explanation as to where the sun went at night described it as being swallowed by the sky goddess in the evening, and being given birth to by her at dawn. Nut was often depicted on the ceiling of burial chambers and inside the lid of sarcophagi, displaying the idea that the dead person, like the sun, would be reborn. It may be that, in the Pyramid Texts, the idea of the dead king passing through the body of the goddess is being expressed in metaphorical terms.

The imperishable stars

The Pyramid Texts imply that the king was believed to join the circumpolar stars in the northern sky – the 'imperishable stars' that never disappear

▲ The ceiling of the burial chamber in the pyramid of Teti is a vault of stars. The Pyramid Texts are inscribed in columns of hieroglyphs on the chamber walls.

from view. In this way these early royal funerary texts equate the dead king with Osiris, the sun and the stars. They also include hymns to the gods and a long list of offerings of food, drink and clothing. These were to be made at the time of the burial and renewed after the king's death, ideally for eternity, because it was believed that they would sustain the king in the Afterlife. ◆

Fifth-Dynasty pyramids

Instead of the solid limestone blocks used for the great monuments erected during the Fourth Dynasty, the pyramids of the Fifth Dynasty were built from small, roughly-dressed stones, but the inner decoration of their burial chambers and funerary complexes was more lavish than ever before.

Coffin Texts

By the Middle Kingdom (c.2055 BC), it was not only kings and queens who were thought to benefit from having funerary texts included in their burials, but also members of the administrative élite. This fortunate minority was not buried in pyramids but in rock-cut tombs. The spells to aid their transition into the Afterlife were recorded in cursive hieroglyphs on the interior walls of their wooden coffins. This accounts for the

▼ *Vignettes in the* Book of Two Ways *show that features of the waterway and landway were guarded by demons brandishing knives. This coffin belonged to Gua, Chief of Physicians. 12th Dynasty.*

origin of the modern term 'Coffin Texts' – although they have also been found on tomb walls, sarcophagi, statues and stelae in offering chapels.

The Book of Two Ways

More than 1,000 Coffin Texts have been collected. They are derived from the body of royal funerary texts known as the Pyramid Texts, with some careful editing and important additions. The chief component of the Coffin Texts is a detailed guidebook to the Afterlife, known as the *Book of Two Ways*. It has been found drawn inside the bottoms of wooden coffins discovered at el-Bersher, the cemetery of Hermopolis Magna, and the cult centre of Thoth, the lunar deity

of scribes and wisdom. The occupant of the coffin was promised an Afterlife like that of the deceased king, and the chance to travel in the sun god's solar barque. But there was a condition: he had to be able to reel off the right spells and a brief rendition of the theology of the sun god Re. At the end of the *Book of Two Ways* we find the pledge:

As for any person who knows this spell, he will be like Re in the east of the sky, like Osiris in the midst of Duat.

Like the king in the Pyramid Texts, the dead person was assured that he would be reborn into the Afterlife, just as the sun rose at dawn above the eastern horizon, and he would become one not only with the sun god but also with Osiris, god of the dead. It would have been a useful *aide-mémoire* for the deceased to have the words of the spells (which he was expected to know by heart) written on the inside of his coffin.

Map of the Afterlife

There are two versions of the *Book of Two Ways*, and both are thought to have been composed at Hermopolis Magna. Both include references to the non-royal deceased becoming stars in the sky, alongside Thoth. The Coffin Texts were accompanied by the earliest known map of the Afterlife, and on it the Mansion of Thoth is located in the Place of Maat. This map was specifically designed to guide the spirit of the deceased on its journey into the Afterlife. Knowledge of the spells and possession of the map meant that the deceased might become an *akh aper* ('equipped spirit').

The map located the Mansion of Osiris and the Field of *Hetep* (the Egyptian paradise), where the deceased might continue to serve Osiris. However, as in the Pyramid Texts, the Heliopolitan

influence is unmistakable because the largest part of the plan indicated the path followed by the sun god on his voyage. First it moved from east to west along a blue waterway through the inner sky, then it went back again from west to east on a black landway through the outer sky. As in the myth of *The Journey of the Sun through the Netherworld*, found on the walls of royal tombs in the Valley of the Kings dating from the New Kingdom (c.1550–c.1069 BC), the Coffin Texts described the path of the sun god (and thus the deceased) as beset by demons, often wielding knives, throw sticks, spears or nets. If trapped by a demon, it was believed that the dead person might be beheaded, hacked to pieces or burned to death. The most dangerous was the giant serpent Apophis, who threatened to devour the sun every day before dawn, and so had to be symbolically destroyed by the sun's entourage every 24 hours. The only way for the spirit of the deceased to safely pass these obstacles (and others such as mounds, rivers, and gates of fire) was by learning their names and characteristics beforehand. ◆

▲ *Eyes painted on the coffin wall allowed the deceased to see out. Middle Kingdom.*

◀ *The inner coffin of the Commander Sepi is painted with a false door beneath the eyes. Middle Kingdom.*

Seeing eyes

Rectangular coffins of the Middle Kingdom were oriented in the tomb with the head to the north. Eyes were painted on the side of the coffin so that the mummy, whose face was positioned behind them, could see out. The body was therefore laid on its left side, facing east towards the rising sun.

Often the eyes were painted above a niched palace façade (*serekh*) design, or a false door, through which the spirit could pass in and out of the coffin.

The Book of the Dead

The end of the Second Intermediate Period (c.1550 BC) witnessed still further democratization of the Afterlife (see *Coffin Texts*), with the emergence of a collection of nearly 200 spells (or chapters). Today these are known as the Book of the Dead, but they were known to the ancient Egyptians as the '*Formulae for Going Forth by Day*'. These funerary texts came to accompany more people to the grave than ever did the Pyramid Texts (a purely royal prerogative) or Coffin Texts, since they were available to anyone who could afford to have them copied. The text was in fact an edited and supplemented version of the Coffin Texts (as the Coffin Texts had been of the Pyramid Texts), which continued to be included in the burials of wealthy people well into the Graeco-Roman Period (332 BC–AD 395).

Although there were 200 or so spells altogether, each burial contained only as many as the deceased or his family chose (or could afford) to have copied. They have mainly been discovered written on papyrus rolls, although certain spells have also been found recorded on coffins, amulets (such as Chapter 30A inscribed on heart scarabs – see *Funerary Amulets*), tomb walls, figurines (for example Chapter 6 on *shabtis* – see *Shabtis*) and statuary.

The papyrus rolls were often placed in the coffin alongside the body, or they might be wrapped up in the mummy bandaging or inserted into a hollowed-out statuette of Ptah-Sokar-Osiris, the Memphite funerary deity, which was then deposited in the tomb along with a range of other funerary goods. These funerary texts were usually written in hieroglyphs, but Books of the Dead in the more cursive scripts, hieratic and demotic, have also survived. The texts were usually accompanied by brightly coloured illustrations or vignettes, ranging from depictions of the amulets to be included in the mummy wrappings to detailed scenes of the Afterlife.

The form of the book

No one copy of the Book of the Dead contained all the spells that were available, although by the Late Period the sequence had become relatively fixed. Egyptologists refer to the spells as numbered 'chapters', following the system imposed in 1842 by Karl Richard Lepsius (1810–84), when he edited the text of the Book of the Dead of Iufankh from the Ptolemaic Period. This example contained 165 chapters. The most significant texts, such as that concerned with the Weighing of the Heart ceremony, were the most lavishly illustrated.

Towards the end of the Ptolemaic Period, the funerary texts grew shorter and the Book of the Dead tended to be replaced by the Book for Breathing or the Book for Out-lasting Eternity. These short compositions could be written on single sheets, to be placed at the head and feet of the deceased. They still provided safeguards for his or her passage into the Afterlife, such as the requisite denial of short-comings for the deceased to present at the Weighing of the Heart ceremony.

▶ *This painted wooden* shabti *from the tomb of Ramesses IV is equipped with a hoe in each hand ready to break up heavy soil in the Afterlife on behalf of the deceased king. 20th Dynasty.*

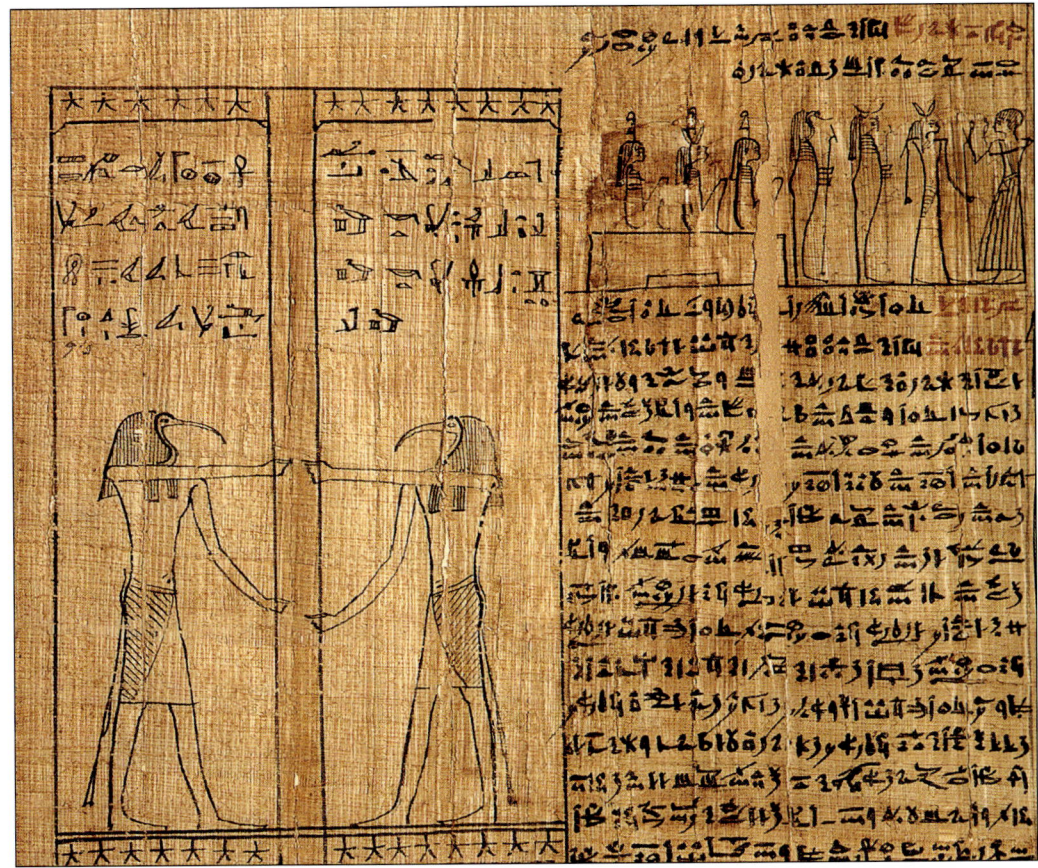

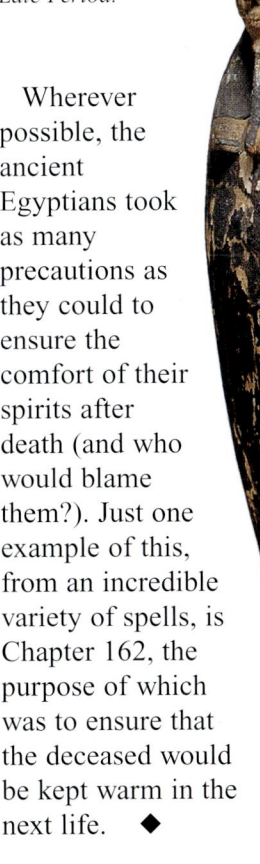

◄ *In the funerary and other religious texts, it is rare to find lines or columns of writing without illustrations alongside. Vignettes tend to accompany the spells throughout the Book of the Dead. These spells in Kahapa's Book of the Dead are written in hieratic, a cursive form of hieroglyphs. Late Period.*

Becoming Osiris

Like the Pyramid Texts of the Old Kingdom (c.2686–c.2181 BC) and the Coffin Texts of the Middle Kingdom (c.2055–c.1650 BC), the main purpose of the Book of the Dead was to provide the deceased person with a collection of spells that would ensure his or her safe passage into the Afterlife. But, unlike the earlier texts, the spells included in the Book of the Dead were dominated by the cult of Osiris, the god of the dead and the Afterlife, rather than that of the sun god Re. Dead people came to be referred to as Osiris, and identification with this god was clearly considered to be the desired goal. It was also Osiris who sat in supreme judgment over the dead, determining their fitness for acceptance into the Afterlife.

Amulets and demons

The texts and their accompanying illustrations provide information on where and when amulets or papyri were to be placed on the body during embalming. Some objects were to be wrapped up in the bandaging, others were to be only temporarily brought into contact with the body. The texts also convey an idea of how the ancient Egyptians imagined the Afterlife they hoped to enter (see *Beliefs about the Afterlife*). As recorded in the Coffin Texts, there were a whole host of threatening demons and other obstacles that stood between the deceased and his or her arrival in 'paradise'. Probably the most crucial section of the Book of the Dead was Chapter 125, which described the final judgment of the dead person before Osiris. His or her lifetime was assessed to check that he or she had behaved well enough to be reborn into the Afterlife (see *The Weighing of the Heart*). If an ancient Egyptian could afford the inclusion of only one chapter of the Book of the Dead in the burial, he or she would have been well advised to choose this one.

▶ *By the Middle Kingdom, Sokar had been syncretized with the gods Ptah and Osiris, and prayers were being addressed to him as a funerary deity. Here, he is accompanied by the Horus falcon. Ptolemaic Period.*

Wherever possible, the ancient Egyptians took as many precautions as they could to ensure the comfort of their spirits after death (and who would blame them?). Just one example of this, from an incredible variety of spells, is Chapter 162, the purpose of which was to ensure that the deceased would be kept warm in the next life. ◆

Funerary Equipment

From Predynastic times (c.5500 BC), the ancient Egyptians chose to include in their burials as much funerary equipment as they could afford. From the Dynastic Period (c.3100 BC), this equipment included the dead person's personal possessions, items made especially for the tomb, ritual objects linked specifically with the funeral and burial, funerary texts (often on papyrus rolls), figurines, statues, coffins, sarcophagi, amulets, food and drink. If the individual concerned was wealthy, as much as possible was included in his or her tomb.

A variety of goods

We know from several sources what was included in burials. First, the objects themselves have been discovered during the excavation of tombs; second, information about the goods to be buried with the dead is provided by the funerary texts; and third, scenes of funeral processions painted on the walls of non-royal tombs, especially during the New

▶ *Osiris boxes (or beds) were planted with grain intended to grow in the tomb. Only seven are known, but associated with them are Osiris bricks and corn mummies.*

Kingdom (c.1550–c.1069 BC), include people carrying a range of goods to the burial.

A selection of funerary goods to accompany the deceased into the Afterlife might have included: a bed with a mattress and a headrest; a couple of chairs and stools with cushions; tables and stands (together with the wine jars to stand in them); boxes and chests; linen clothing, wigs, sandals, walking-sticks and staffs of office; draw-neck bags; stone vessels; jewellery; mirrors; fans; and boardgames. In some cases, equipment related to the dead person's profession was included. For example, a scribe might be buried with his scribal equipment; a painter with his brushes, paints and the string he used to mark out a grid with which to proportion figures; and a soldier with his weapons, shield, horse and chariot.

Magical paraphernalia

Much of the equipment placed in the tomb would have been objects of daily use, still familiar to us

◀ *The circular end of the funerary cones found in New Kingdom tombs may have represented the sun as part of the solar iconography of rebirth.*

all. But there would also have been a considerable number of magical and ritual items, some of which would have been inscribed with spells or details about the deceased. From the Late Period (c.747 BC), a flat disc made of bronze or cartonnage (plaster-stiffened linen), known as a *hypocephalus*, was placed under the head of the mummy. It was inscribed with vignettes of various gods and the text of Chapter 162 of the Book of the

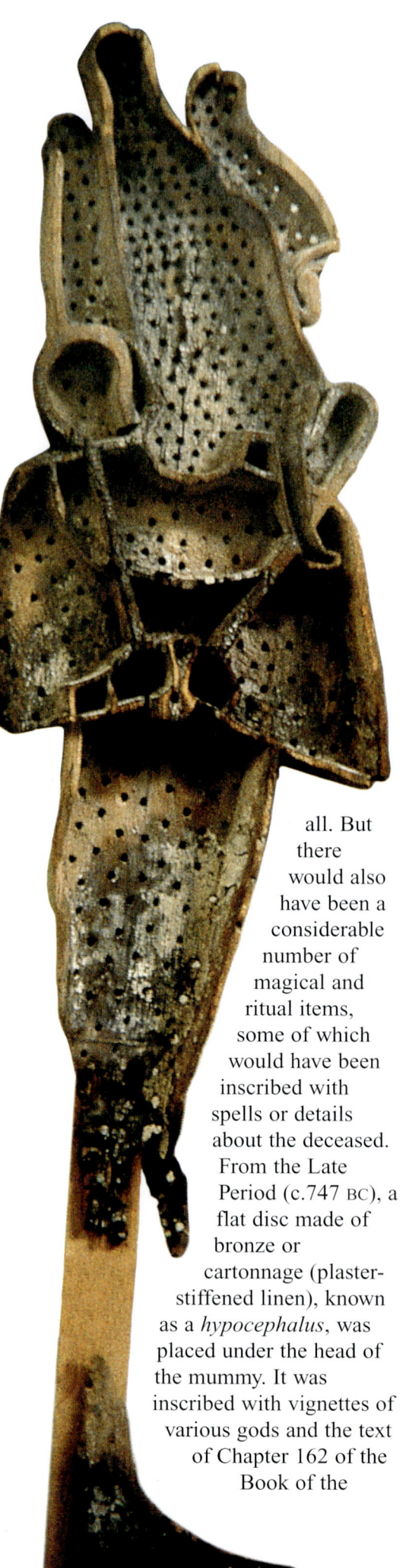

▲ *About 30 'reserve heads' have been found, all from private mastaba-tombs in the Memphite necropolis (mainly at Giza), and primarily from the reigns of Khufu and Khafre. 4th Dynasty.*

Dead, the purpose of which was to ensure that the deceased would be kept warm in the Afterlife.

Some New Kingdom tombs in the Theban area had as many as 300 'funerary cones' at their entrances. These were made of clay, and measured 10–15cm (4–6in) in length. Their flat circular end was usually stamped with the name, title, and sometimes a short inscription or genealogy of the tomb owner, in hieroglyphs. Although these were not necessarily found *in situ*, their tapering ends were probably set in plaster, with only their broad ends visible.

Symbols and amulets

Some types of funerary equipment have been found in tombs from a particular period of Egyptian history. During the Old Kingdom (c.2686–c.2181 BC), for example, a roughly life-sized model stone head, referred to as a 'reserve head', was placed near the entrance to the burial chamber. Its function was probably to serve as a substitute head for the deceased in the event of his or her actual one being destroyed after burial (perhaps by tomb robbers). During the New

Kingdom, an Osiris-shaped box might be deposited in the burial chamber. This was filled with Nile silt and planted with grain, which was watered and was intended to sprout in the darkness of the tomb. This 'Osiris box' would have emphasized the role of Osiris as god of the dead, rebirth and vegetation, and the sprouting of the grain would have symbolized the rebirth of the deceased into the Afterlife.

Also during this period of Egyptian history, four 'magic bricks' of unbaked mud were set on the four sides of the tomb. Each brick had an amulet inserted in it: the one beside the western wall had a faience *djed*-pillar (see *Funerary Amulets*); the one by the eastern wall incorporated an unfired clay figure of the god Anubis; the one by the southern wall contained a reed with a wick, resembling a torch; and the one by the northern wall contained a mummiform *shabti*-like figure. The bricks were inscribed with sections of Chapter 151 of the Book of the Dead, which described the role they played in protecting the dead person against the evil enemies of Osiris. Their positions guarded against such an approach from any of the four cardinal directions. ◆

Imiut

Certain objects that were placed in the tomb were closely associated with a particular deity. One example is the model of an *imiut*, discovered in the tomb of the Eighteenth-Dynasty ruler Tutankhamun (c.1336–c.1327 BC). The *imiut* was a fetish of the cult of Anubis, the jackal-headed god of embalming and cemeteries. It consisted of the headless skin of an animal (usually a feline), which was inflated or stuffed and tied to a pole in a pot.

Funerary Amulets

Amulets were positioned in specific places on the dead body, held in place by the mummy wrappings. Their function was to protect the dead person, and it appears that the greater the number included in the bandaging, the greater the degree of protection they afforded. Often, as many as several hundred amulets have been found on one body. A list of 104 funerary amulets can be found on a doorway in a complex of rooms dedicated to Osiris, in the Temple of Hathor at Dendera.

Sections of both the Coffin Texts and the Book of the Dead are concerned with instructions detailing where and when amulets or papyri should be placed on the body during the embalming process. Some of these objects were to be wrapped up in the bandaging, while others were to be brought into contact with the body temporarily to enable their magical properties to take effect. Pictures of certain amulets might also be drawn on the bandaging.

The ideal, for those who could afford it, was to have a huge variety of different amulets made of precious stones and metals. Amulets that had been worn during life incorporated in items of jewellery were often included in the burial. Of particular importance were the golden vulture collar, the scarab worn over the heart and the Eye of Horus. Chapter 157 of the Book of the Dead was the 'spell for the vulture of gold placed at the throat of the deceased'. The vulture was an incarnation of the protective mother goddess Isis, who kept her son Horus safe within her large encircling wings.

▶ *Four ancient Egyptian words are translated as 'amulet':* meket, nehet *and* sa *derive from verbs meaning 'to guard' or 'to protect', and* wedja *has the same sound as the word meaning 'wellbeing'.*

▶ *The protective Eye of Horus amulet was probably used in greater numbers on mummies than any other amulet. It is first found in the late Old Kingdom, and continued in use until the Roman Period. This glazed-composition example dates from c.600 BC.*

The scarab beetle

The protective amulet for the heart was in the form of the scarab beetle, the manifestation of the creator and solar deity Khepri. It was a symbol of new life and resurrection. The scarab beetle was seen to push a ball of mud along the ground, and from this came the idea of the beetle rolling the sun across the sky. Subsequently, the young beetles were observed to hatch from their eggs inside the ball of mud, hence the idea of creation: life springing forth from primordial mud.

The heart scarab was a large scarab amulet which was wrapped in the mummy bandaging over the deceased's heart. It was made out of a range of green and dark-coloured materials, including glazed stearite, schist, feldspar, haematite and obsidian. It was inscribed with Chapter 30 of the Book of the Dead. The gist of the inscription was an instruction from the dead person to his or her heart that, when it was brought before the tribunal of the gods led by Osiris for judgment, it should not confess to any of the wrongs that the dead person might have committed during his or her lifetime (see *The Weighing of the Heart*). As a further precaution, heart-shaped amulets might

The sign of the embalmer

An amulet in the shape of two fingers was placed on the left side of the mummy's pelvis, and it is possible that it symbolized the two fingers of the chief embalmer.

also be included in the bandaging, to ensure that the heart remained at all times in the body (except during the actual Weighing of the Heart ceremony). Chapter 29B of the Book of the Dead stated that these amulets should be made of cornelian, but they have also been found made of other materials, such as glass.

Amulets and the gods

The Eye of Horus (the *udjat*- or *wadjat*-eye, literally 'the eye which is whole or sound') was an amulet in the shape of an eye. It was placed over the incision usually cut in the left side of the abdomen of a dead body for the removal of the internal organs. In one version of the myth of Osiris, his son Horus offered his healed eye to his dead

father, and it was such a powerful charm that it brought Osiris back to life. The myth of *The Contendings of Horus and Seth* tells us that Horus had his eyesight cured, and so his eye symbolized healing and the process of making whole. The Eye of Horus was used as a protective amulet, symbolizing in particular strength and perfection.

A whole range of other amulets were also included in burials. The detailed instructions accompanying the spells in the Book of the Dead often specified the material out of which the amulet should be made, whether or not it should be strung, and if so the type of stringing to be used. They also specified exactly where on the

◀ *The* djed-*pillar may originally have represented a stylized tree-trunk with the branches lopped off. It is first known to have been used as an amulet in the late Old Kingdom. Ptolemaic Period.*

body the amulet should be placed, and at which stage of the mummification process this should be done.

The *djed*-pillar amulet was associated with Osiris, god of the dead and the Afterlife (it has been interpreted as his backbone), and was thought to symbolize stability. Chapter 155 of the Book of the Dead contains:

...words to be spoken over a djed-*pillar of gold, strung upon a fibre of sycamore...and placed at the throat of the deceased on the day of burial.*

Another amulet associated with Osiris was the staircase amulet, which represented the stepped dais where his throne stood.

The *tyet*-amulet was a protective amulet associated with the goddess Isis. It was knot-shaped and may have represented the knotted girdle of the goddess, or perhaps a tampon inserted into Isis when she was pregnant. This was

done so that she would not miscarry or so that her wicked brother Seth could not harm the son she was carrying. Chapter 156 of the Book of the Dead specified that the *tyet*-amulet should be made of red jasper (the colour of the blood of Isis).

Chapters 159 and 160 were to be said over a *wadj*-amulet made of green feldspar. The ancient Egyptian word for 'green' was in fact *wadj*, and this amulet was in the shape of a single stem and flower of papyrus. In a funerary context its purpose was to ensure that the deceased enjoyed eternal youth.

Models and tiny figures

Other amulets included the headrest amulet, to ensure the head of the deceased would be eternally raised up (like the sun that rose each day); the animal-headed *was*-sceptre amulet, which granted well being and prosperity; the mason's plummet amulet, which guaranteed perpetual

▲ *Amulets such as the* djed-*pillar,* ankh *and heart amulet, as well as figures of deities, were included in the decoration of coffins.*

equilibrium; and the carpenter's square amulet, which guaranteed eternal rectitude.

Amulets of small figures of deities such as the scorpion-goddess Selket and the jackal-god Anubis, were also included for protection. Tiny models of parts of the body seem to have endowed the deceased with their properties – such as action, movement or use of the senses – and could act as substitutes if the real parts went missing. Models of animals were also considered of magical use for granting the deceased the particular characteristics associated with them: for example, the virility of a bull or ram, the speed of a hare or the fertility of a cow, cat or frog. More enigmatically, a serpent's head made out of a red material was believed to ensure cool refreshment for the throat. ◆

Shabtis

From the Middle Kingdom (c.2055 BC), the ancient Egyptians were buried with small human statuettes known as *shabti*-figures, an incredible number of which have come to light over the years. They were usually mummiform, and were made out of faience, stone, wood, pottery, bronze, wax or glass. They were inscribed with Chapter 6 of the Book of the Dead. This was a spell to ensure that the *shabti*, and not the deceased, would end up doing any hard work that he or she might be called upon to do in the Afterlife:

▼ *One type of* shabti-*box had a vaulted lid and raised ends. During the 19th Dynasty a multiple form appeared with a dividing partition.*

O shabti, *if the deceased is called upon to do any of the work required there in the necropolis at any time…you shall say, 'Here I am. I will do it.'*

By the Late Period (c.747 BC), the term *shabti* (and the variant *shawabti*) had been largely replaced by the word *ushabti*, meaning 'answerer'. Now the emphasis in the spell was very much on the role of the figure to answer instead of the dead person when his or her name was called. The hard toil anticipated was that of food production – the funerary text specifies the preparation of the land ready for cultivation, the irrigation of the fields, and the clearing of sand from east to west. To ensure the efficiency of

▶ *During the Ramesside and Third Intermediate Periods the overseer* (reis) shabtis, *who were sometimes referred to as 'chiefs of ten', were represented in living form, as in this faience figure from Memphis, while their workforce were represented as mummiform. 22nd Dynasty.*

these figurines, during the early New Kingdom (c.1550 BC), they were sometimes equipped with a model hoe and basket, and later on they were modelled holding these tools.

By the New Kingdom a person might be buried with as many as 365 *shabtis* – one for every day of the year – accompanied by a further 36 'overseers'. From the Third Intermediate Period (c.1069 BC), these 'overseer figures' were sometimes equipped with whips to make absolutely sure that the workers performed their tasks quickly and satisfactorily. The growing numbers of *shabtis* made it necessary for them to be stored in special *shabti*-boxes. ◆

Canopic Jars

Canopic jars were the containers used to hold the internal organs that were removed from the body before mummification and embalmed separately. During the Old Kingdom (c.2686–c.2181 BC), when mummification was in its infancy, the jars that served this purpose were stone vessels with flat lids. It was not until the First Intermediate Period (c.2181–c.2055 BC) that the four jars each acquired a human-headed

stopper. From this time, too, the packages of viscera placed inside them were sometimes decorated with human-faced masks. Then from the late Eighteenth Dynasty onwards, the stoppers of the jars were each shaped like the head of one of the minor funerary deities known as the 'Four Sons of Horus'. These were the baboon-headed Hapy, the human-headed Imsety, the jackal-headed Duamutef, and the falcon-headed Qebehsenuef.

The Sons of Horus

It was the job of these four deities to protect the internal organs of the deceased. These would have been removed from the body, embalmed, anointed and wrapped in linen ready to be placed in the jars for safe keeping,

◄ *The use of stone and ceramic canopic jars seems to have come to an end around the beginning of the Ptolemaic Period (332 BC). This limestone jar belonged to Prince Hornakht (c.850–c.825 BC) of the 22nd Dynasty.*

▲ *By the New Kingdom (c.1550–c.1069 BC) the Four Sons of Horus had become members of the group known as the 'seven blessed ones' who were said to guard Osiris's coffin in the northern sky. They are shown here on the wall of Queen Nefertari's tomb in west Thebes. 19th Dynasty.*

because the ancient Egyptians firmly believed that the deceased required his or her organs in order to be reborn into the Afterlife. Hapy guarded the lungs, Imsety the liver, Duamutef the stomach and upper intestines, and Qebehsenuef the lower intestines.

The ancient Egyptians went to such great lengths to ensure the preservation of the entire body for the Afterlife that each of the four organs, together with the Son of Horus who was its particular guardian deity, was under the further protection of four of the most important of the Egyptian goddesses, who guarded the jars themselves: Nephthys protected the jar containing the lungs, Isis the jar containing the liver, Neith the jar containing the stomach and upper

▲ *By the late Middle Kingdom (c.1650 BC), a set of canopic equipment might consist of a carved stone outer chest and a wooden inner one holding the four jars. This jar stopper belonged to the canopic equipment of Nefertari. 19th Dynasty.*

was placed in a niche in the burial chamber, close to the coffin.

The ancient Egyptians upheld their longstanding funerary traditions and continued to include canopic jars in their burials, but from the Twenty-first Dynasty (c.1069 BC) the jars were no longer functioning receptacles, in that they were left empty, or were not hollowed out, so their presence in the tomb became purely symbolic. Although the internal organs were still removed for the actual embalming of the body, they were no longer entombed separately but were packaged and returned to the body for burial. The Four Sons of Horus, in the amuletic form of wax figures, were also often inserted into the body together with the packaged organs. ◆

intestines, and Selket the jar containing the lower intestines. These four goddesses were also associated with the four cardinal points: north, south, east and west, respectively.

In the Pyramid Texts of the Old Kingdom, the Four Sons of Horus were described as the 'friends of the king' because they were said to assist him in his ascent into the sky. In funerary art, for example in tomb paintings and vignettes of the Book of the Dead on papyrus, the Four Sons of Horus occurred as small mummified human figures with their respective heads. They were often depicted close to Osiris, sometimes standing on an open lotus blossom. They might also be included as amulets in the burial – these took the form of small modelled figures of mummified human bodies, again with their respective heads.

Empty jars

By the late Middle Kingdom (c.1650 BC), the set of four canopic jars were commonly stored in a wooden chest which in turn was placed inside a stone outer chest. The whole ensemble

Canopus of Osiris

The term 'canopic jar' is actually a misnomer arrived at by early Egyptologists. They considered that the jars resembled the form in which Osiris, the god of the dead and the Afterlife, was worshipped in the Delta city of Canopus – a port on the Mediterranean coast. The city is said to have been named after the pilot of the ship belonging to the Greek hero Menelaus. According to Homer, Menelaus died on the Egyptian coast after a storm wrecked his ship on his way home after the Trojan wars.

This manifestation of Osiris as a human-headed jar with a foot and a swollen belly was referred to as the 'Canopus of Osiris'. The form has been found on some Roman coins minted at Alexandria, so it must have been a fairly well-known image during at least the Roman period of Egyptian history.

Coffins and Sarcophagi

During the Early Dynastic period, (c.3100–c.2686), if the ancient Egyptians did not bury their dead in direct contact with the sand they used baskets, large pots or square crates. This did not interfere with the age-old tradition of burying the dead in the foetal position. But with the advent of effective artificial preservation of dead bodies, the corpses had to be stretched out to facilitate the removal of the internal organs, and so wooden coffins became full-length and rectangular in shape. By the end of the Old Kingdom (c.2181 BC), food offerings were often painted on the inside of the coffin, in order to provide symbolic sustenance for the *ka* of the deceased (see *Tomb Scenes and Models*). Two eyes were painted or carved on one of the longer sides of the coffin at the head end so that the deceased might magically be able to look out through them. This followed from the ancient Egyptian belief that the dead had their faculties returned to them at the 'Opening of the Mouth' ceremonies (see *Funerals*). The coffin was positioned in the tomb so that the eyes faced east – the place of the living and the rising Sun. These eyes were *udjat*-eyes (or Eyes of Horus), so they symbolized completeness, well being, strength and perfection.

Decoration and design

Royalty and the wealthiest people were buried in sarcophagi of granite, basalt, limestone or calcite, some of which were carved with a design known as a *serekh*. This was a pattern of recessed panelling thought perhaps to imitate the architecture of the earliest royal palaces. The design can also be found painted on wooden coffins.

By the beginning of the Middle Kingdom (c.2055) the key features of the coffins of the higher echelons of society were the Coffin Texts and maps of the Afterlife which were painted on the interior walls and bases (see *Coffin*

◄ *The* rishi *coffin of Nubkheperre Intef was made from a hollowed-out log overlaid with gilded gesso. 17th Dynasty.*

▼ *The stone sarcophagus of King Amenhotep II, carved in the shape of a cartouche, decorated with divine figures and an eye-panel. 18th Dynasty.*

▲ *Many coffins and sarcophagi of later periods, such as that of the priest Ken-Hor (c.750 BC) were made in the shape of the* Per-nu *or Lower Egyptian shrine.*

Texts). Those who could afford it were buried in an inner rectangular coffin placed inside an outer one, both of which would have been made from well-cut planks of imported timber. Anything imported was regarded as a luxury item and thus an indicator of wealth and a symbol of status. The timber native to Egypt was decidedly more flimsy than, for example, the cedarwood that could be imported from the Lebanon. Poorer people naturally had no choice but to use the local timber, such as sycamore or tamarisk, in their burials, and it was often roughly cut with attempts made to disguise it using a coating of plaster.

The Middle Kingdom also saw the emergence of the anthropoid coffin. This appears to have been regarded as a substitute for the body itself, in case the body was destroyed at some stage after burial. Anthropoid coffins were usually made of cartonnage (layers of linen stiffened with plaster) rather than wood, but were placed inside a rectangular wooden outer coffin.

A rather beautiful type of anthropoid coffin appeared at Thebes late in the Second Intermediate Period (c.1650–c.1550 BC). The surface was covered in a pattern of feathers (hence the name *rishi*, from the Arabic word for 'feathered'). This was possibly to indicate that the body was being protected by the enveloping wings of a vulture – a manifestation of the mother goddesses Mut and Isis. Alternatively, it may have

been intended to represent the *ba* – the personality or moral essence – of the deceased, which was symbolized as a bird with a human head.

The anthropoid coffins of the Eighteenth Dynasty (c.1550–c.1295 BC) displayed another new feature – the arms on the coffins were carved in high relief. They were usually depicted crossed over the chest like those of the god Osiris, and some coffins had modelled beards like Osiris. These coffins tended to be covered in depictions of deities, with bands of hieroglyphic extracts from the funerary texts. By the Ramesside Period (the Nineteenth and Twentieth Dynasties, c.1295–c.1069 BC), the fashion was to bury the dead inside a nest of anthropoid wooden coffins, which for royalty and noblemen might sit inside an outermost stone sarcophagus. Then by the Twenty-second Dynasty (c.945–c.715 BC) it became usual for the innermost of the coffins to be made of cartonnage with a wooden footboard.

The goddess Nut

Nut, the sky goddess, was closely associated with coffins and sarcophagi. From the late New Kingdom onwards this goddess was often depicted stretched out inside the lid. She was believed to swallow the sun in the evening and give birth to it at dawn. In keeping with the solar aspect of funerary religion, the deceased was believed to be reborn from her (and thus the coffin or sarcophagus) into the Afterlife. ◆

Sarcophagi

The term 'sarcophagus' is derived from the Greek word for 'flesh-eater'. This reflects the Hellenic belief that the type of stone used to make coffins actually consumed their contents.

Tomb Scenes and Models

For the ancient Egyptians, two- and three-dimensional representation and the written word were charged with magical potency, especially within the context of the tomb and temple or chapel. They believed that by depicting something they might magically animate it and make it happen, at least in symbolic terms. But the ancient Egyptians were also a rational and realistic people. They knew that family, friends and passers-by (or the priesthoods of funerary cults if they were particularly important members of society), would eventually give up leaving food offerings at the tombs or associated funerary chapels, so they took further precautions to provide magical substitutes for the actual food supplies. Tomb reliefs, paintings and models representing agriculture and food

▲ *The hieroglyphs beneath Nebamun's raised arm in this fragment of wall painting from his tomb describe him as 'taking recreation and seeing what is good in the place of eternity'. 18th Dynasty.*

production served to ensure an adequate and eternal supply of food and drink for the *ka* of the deceased in the Afterlife. The images were expected to work their magic in conjunction with the '*hetep-di-nesw* ('an offering which the king gives') formula'. This was a prayer inscribed on funerary furniture such as coffins, stelae and the false doors in tombs which served as a link between the worlds of the living and the dead. It asked for the king to placate the funerary deity Osiris or Anubis with gifts on behalf of the deceased, and then for offerings such as bread, beer and linen to be made to the *ka* of the dead

person. During the First Intermediate Period and Middle Kingdom (c.2181–c.1650 BC), 'soul houses' were often included in the burials of less wealthy people. These were pottery houses (often quite crudely modelled), with courtyards covered in models of food offerings.

Scenes of daily activity, agriculture and food production occurred on the walls of non-royal tombs throughout Egyptian history. Painted limestone figurines of servants brewing beer, grinding corn and so on, have been found in burials dating to the late Old Kingdom (c.2686–c.2181 BC). Of particular note, because of their superb craftsmanship and the incredible number that have survived, are the wooden tomb models of the Middle Kingdom (c.2055 – c.1650 BC). The most famous of these models were discovered in the tomb of

▼ *'Soul houses' (symbolic homes for the* kas *of the dead) were placed beside the mouths of shaft-burials. Middle Kingdom.*

the Eleventh-Dynasty chancellor Meketre (c.2000 BC) at Deir el-Bahri. They are now in the Cairo Museum and include absolutely exquisite models of a weavers' and a carpenters' workshop, a butcher, a bakery, boats, a cattle count, and two models of Meketre's house and garden with trees and a pool.

Imagining the Afterlife

The people who were able to afford the extreme luxury of a decorated tomb were highly unlikely ever to have actually toiled on the land. But in a funerary context they were depicted ploughing the land, sowing seeds and reaping the harvest. The emphasis was clearly on the fundamental principle of the importance of an individual's relationship with, and acknowledgement of, his dependence on the fertile silt of the Nile Valley. To ensure that the deceased would not really have to perform these tasks in the Afterlife, they included *shabti*-figures in their burials to do the work for them.

The hope appears to have been that the Afterlife was like this life, but free from worry and hard work. Paintings and reliefs portrayed the tomb owner and his wife, family and friends enjoying themselves at parties and various leisure activities, such as hunting hippopotami or waterfowl. Such scenes were laden with symbolism, particularly connected with fertility and the suppression of

▶ *Models showed the production of food, such as this woman grinding barley, using a saddle quern and rubbing stone, to make bread and beer.*

▶ *The false door was a stone or wooden imitation doorway which first appeared in tombs of the Old Kingdom. It was usually carved with a figure of the deceased seated before an offering table. Here the dead man is Sheshi.*

evil or chaos. Symbols of sexuality and fertility (the two being considered far more interconnected by the ancient Egyptians than by us today) such as ducks, monkeys, cats, heavy wigs, almost transparent clothing, and vegetation crop up in the scenes. The ancient Egyptian terms for some of the activities portrayed are also worth considering in this context, for the verb 'to throw a throwstick' (*qema*) is the same as that for 'to father a child' or 'to create', and the verb 'to harpoon' (*seti*) is the same as that for 'to impregnate'.

Idealized portrayals

The portrayal of the tomb owner hunting birds, hippopotami and crocodiles (or wild bulls and lions in the case of kings) showed him taking part in activities that he had probably enjoyed during his lifetime and hoped to enjoy in the Afterlife. But it was also the display of the deceased as a good man who had been assessed as 'true of voice' at the divine tribunal (see *The Weighing of the Heart*), overcoming symbols of evil or chaos, as Horus had conquered Seth in *The Contendings of Horus and Seth*.

At all times, the style and content of the artistic representation was extremely idealized. The tomb owner was always shown as strong and athletic, even if he had died in extreme old age,

and his wife was always young and slender despite the fact that giving birth to many children had no doubt wreaked havoc with her body. But anyone who could afford such scenes in their tombs chose to be depicted in this idealized way in the hope that this would indeed be how they might look in the Afterlife.

The Book of the Dead

From the New Kingdom (c.1550 BC) onwards, scenes from the Book of the Dead also appeared. By depicting the funerary rituals taking place it was hoped that they would happen after death. When representing the dead person's heart balancing against the feather of Maat at the Weighing of the Heart ceremony, it was believed that, magically, this would occur. It was as though portraying the deceased and his family in the Afterlife would guarantee entry into paradise. ◆

Funerals

We know how the ancient Egyptians conducted their funerals because they depicted the proceedings on the walls of their tombs during the New Kingdom (c.1550–c.1069 BC). The most detailed portrayals of events are to be found in non-royal tombs.

The mummy passed in procession from the embalming house to the tomb, the attendant grandeur depending on the wealth and status of the individual concerned. The mummy usually lay in an open booth shaped like a shrine and bedecked with funerary bouquets. This was mounted on a boat-shaped bier which in turn sat on a sled drawn by oxen. A priest walked in front of the bier, sprinkling milk and burning incense. The canopic chest was dragged or carried behind the bier. All manner of funerary goods and food offerings were also carried in the procession, destined for burial alongside the body. One of the more enigmatic components of the procession was the *tekenu*, a human-headed sack-like object usually depicted in wall paintings and reliefs being drawn by cattle on a sled. Its significance is very uncertain but it has been suggested that this was a sack containing those parts of the body that were not actually mummified or placed in the canopic jars, but were nevertheless regarded as essential for the rebirth of the deceased into the Afterlife.

Mourning the deceased

Professional female mourners dressed in pale blue were an important presence at every funeral. They let down their hair and tore at it, bared and beat their breasts, wept, wailed and threw dirt from the ground over themselves. The two chief mourners were often identified with the goddesses Isis and Nephthys who, according to mythology, had pieced together the body of their brother Osiris (whose dead body had been hacked apart

by their wicked brother Seth), mummified it, and mourned his death. Just as Osiris had been mummified in order to preserve his body and had then been reborn, it was expected that the deceased and mummified person would be reborn into the Afterlife. Dancers also accompanied the procession. These were the *muu*-dancers, who wore kilts and tall white headdresses, rather like the White

▲ *The strict conventions of Egyptian art allowed women to be depicted displaying hysterical behaviour, such as these mourners in the tomb of Ramose, but men had at all times to be portrayed as upright and in control. 18th Dynasty.*

▼ *This vignette from the Book of the Dead of Ani is one of a series of scenes illustrating the role of the* ba *after death. Here the* ba *is united with the body of the deceased.*

▲ *A number of different ritual implements were used in the Opening of the Mouth ceremony (shown here on the papyrus Book of the Dead of Hunefer). Their use was believed to restore the dead person's ability to see, breathe, eat and drink. 19th Dynasty.*

Crown of Upper Egypt. There were also priests, distinguished by their shaven heads.

The key rituals performed at the funeral were the final act of purifying the mummified body with water (probably a natron solution) and incense; the anointing of the mummy with sacred oils; and the ceremony known as the Opening of the Mouth. This was considered vital for restoring the senses to the dead person so he or she could be reborn into the Afterlife, and so the body could become the vessel for the *ka* (spirit) of the deceased. This rite was also performed on any statues of the deceased, as well as the cult statues placed in shrines and temples throughout Egypt, thereby animating the statues as vessels for the divine presence of the various deities. It was originally the eldest son's responsibility to carry out this act so that his parent could live

on after death, which explains why the ancient Egyptians considered infertility such a desperate problem. However, during the New Kingdom a new priestly function developed – that of the *sem*-priest, who is depicted in the tomb paintings and vignettes from the Book of the Dead wearing a leopardskin, and performing the Opening of the Mouth ceremony. In the tomb of the Eighteenth-Dynasty king Tutankhamun (c.1336–c.1327 BC) there is a depiction on the wall of the Opening of the Mouth of the deceased pharaoh. It is being performed by his chief official, the vizier Ay, who had himself portrayed in the role of the king's heir in order to legitimize his unlawful claim to the throne. Ay did indeed succeed to the throne and ruled Egypt for about four years (c.1327–c.1323 BC).

It is known that during the New Kingdom this ceremony consisted of 75 separate acts, involving the touching of the mouth, eyes, ears, nose and other parts of the body with a variety of different ritual implements. These included a *pesesh-kaf* (a fishtail-shaped flint knife), a chisel, an adze, a *netjeri*-blade (usually made of meteoric iron), a

rod ending in a snake's head, and the right leg of an ox which would have been specially butchered for the occasion.

Interring the body

All stages of the funeral were accompanied by recitation from the funerary texts (especially the Book of the Dead) by a Lector Priest (who would also have recited the spells during the embalming and mummification of the body). The gist of these utterances was the successful rebirth of the dead person and his or her continued and comfortable existence in the Afterlife. The final offerings made to the spirit of the deceased included natron, incense, eye-paint (malachite or galena), linen, food and drink, as well as the foreleg and heart of a bull.

The mummy was placed inside its coffin, often part of a nest of coffins, which was deposited in the burial chamber together with the canopic chest, food supplies for the deceased and other funerary equipment. Magic bricks (see *Funerary Equipment*) were positioned around the coffin or sarcophagus, and after these extensive and elaborate proceedings the body was left in peace as the tomb was sealed. The waste material from the embalming process was not considered pure enough to bury with the body, but it was still thought to be important to the deceased's existence in the Afterlife, so it was buried nearby.

After the burial, the family and guests sat down at portable tables set up outside the tomb to enjoy a feast of all kinds of food, wine and beer. ◆

Tombs

The ancient Egyptian tomb, whether a pyramid or a shallow pit, was considered the eternal resting-place for the body and funerary goods, both of which were believed vital for rebirth and survival in the Afterlife.

Because towns and villages were built of mudbrick and were situated within the floodplain, very few have survived. Our understanding of ancient Egypt thus relies heavily on the information gleaned from tombs, which were built to last for eternity. Wherever possible they were built of stone or were cut into the natural rock, and they were located on the desert fringes, where they avoided the ravages of the Nile flood. In this hot, dry setting they have survived to this day, and often the painted decoration on their walls still looks fresh and vibrant.

The most splendid monuments were luxuries that only the king, his family and officials, and the wealthiest members of society could afford. Each tomb had a burial chamber, but of equal if not greater importance was the associated 'offering chapel', where it was hoped food offerings would continue to be left for the deceased to ensure a continued existence in the Afterlife. By the New Kingdom (c.1550 BC), the tombs of the pharaohs in the Valley of the Kings each had a mortuary temple as grand as any of the temples dedicated to the most eminent of Egyptian deities.

◀ *The Step Pyramid Complex of King Djoser is Egypt's earliest monumental stone structure.*

Mastabas

Important early royal tombs have been discovered at the cemetery sites of Abydos and Saqqara. These were the burials of the rulers of the First and Second Dynasties (c.3100–c.2686 BC), and those of members of their family and administration. The size and complexity of some of these tombs indicates the increased wealth, control of manpower and organization of the Early Dynastic kings and their governments. They provide us with evidence for the initial stages of building on a monumental scale, and the emergence of a distinct architectural symbolism, especially regarding funerary beliefs and kingship.

Because of their shape, these early tombs are called mastabas, from the Arabic word for 'bench'. They consisted of brick chambers (the central one being the burial chamber) in pits dug in the desert or – by the end of the Second Dynasty – excavated out of the actual bedrock. The pit was covered by a simple superstructure in the form of a plain square or rectangular enclosure, its outer wall often recessed in imitation of a palace façade. This enclosure was filled with sand and gravel, or

sometimes contained storage chambers or magazines, covering an area of up to 340sq m (410sq yd).

The evidence concerning exactly which of the kings was buried at which of the two sites is a little shaky, and disagreement continues. But it is generally held today that all the kings of the First Dynasty and the last two of the Second Dynasty (Peribsen and Khasekhemwy) were laid to rest at Abydos. Their tombs were marked by pairs of free-standing stone stelae similar to gravestones, bearing the name of the king in a *serekh* design, usually surmounted by the image of the god Horus in falcon form. The other Second Dynasty rulers were buried at Saqqara, on the northern spur of the desert plateau there. This was the cemetery of the administrative capital, Memphis, and so it makes sense that the great administrators were also buried there, in a manner similar to that of the kings.

Funerary palaces

The subterranean chambers of these early tombs were often lined with wooden panelling – a clear indication of long-distance trade, because the ancient Egyptians had no native timber suitable for such a purpose. From the mid-First Dynasty (c.2950 BC), a stairway paved with blocks of granite led to the burial chamber, providing evidence for quarrying in the region of Aswan in the far south of Egypt. At the same time, fine quality limestone was being used in the tombs at Saqqara, quarried across the river at Tura. The threat of tomb robbers was obviously already a concern, even at this very early stage of Egyptian history, because security measures such as portcullises were already in place.

At Abydos each tomb was associated with a separate building, sometimes referred to as a funerary palace, which was situated closer to the cultivation and

▲ *While the* serekh *of King Djet (shown here on a stela from his tomb at Abydos) was surmounted by the falcon Horus, the* serekh *of Peribsen was surmounted by the Seth animal, and that of Khasekhemwy by both Horus and Seth. Early Dynastic Period.*

water supplies. It is very likely that these buildings served a purpose similar to that of the later mortuary chapels and temples. They housed the *ka* of the deceased in a statue and were the focus of the dead person's funerary cult. As such, offerings and votive material such as stelae inscribed with offering formulae (see *Tomb Scenes and Models*) were placed in them. The best-preserved of these structures belonged to the last ruler of the Second Dynasty, Khasekhemwy (c.2686 BC). It is now called Shunet ez-Zebib ('Storehouse of Raisins'), so it has obviously served a more secular function in its time. It appears to have been enormous: its outer

Osiris's burial place

Later in Egyptian history Abydos became the chief cult centre of Osiris, the deity most associated with the dead and the Afterlife, and according to legend it was his burial place. The early dynastic cemetery at Abydos was situated in the desert at a site now known as Umm el Qa'ab or 'Mother of Pots'. It is so-called because of the vast quantity of pots and sherds that have been found there. These are the remains of offerings made mainly during the New Kingdom (c.1550– c.1069 BC).

▲ *Djoser's Step Pyramid began life as an almost square mastaba (the outline of which is still visible). This was extended to provide a superstructure for a further eleven burial shafts. A four-stepped pyramid and then a final six steps were added over this structure.*

enclosure measured 54 x 113m (177 x 370 ft) and the inner wall still stands 11m (36ft) high in places and is 5.5m (18ft) thick.

At Saqqara, by the end of the First Dynasty (c.2890 BC), the architects chose to combine the two elements of a tomb and a funerary palace in a single structure, with a mortuary chapel on the north side. This feature continued into the Third Dynasty (c.2686–c.2613 BC) on the north face of the earliest pyramid, the Step Pyramid of King Djoser (c.2667–c.2648 BC).

Both the royal tombs and the funerary palaces were surrounded by rows of simple graves. These were marked by stelae, which tell us that these dead people had been members of the royal entourage. Many were women, but there were also minor palace staff, craftsmen, court dwarfs and the king's favourite dogs. It is impossible to be absolutely certain, but it does seem that some of these retainers died just before the royal tomb was closed, raising the question of

human sacrifice. In the case of the First Dynasty king Djer, as many as 580 retainers were buried around his tomb. Were these people killed to accompany and serve the king after his death? If so, this custom did not survive into the Old Kingdom (c.2686–c.2181 BC), when the royal entourage was replaced by models of servants performing tasks, and later by *shabti* figures.

Boat burials and bulls' heads

The mastabas at Saqqara have survived better than those at Abydos, and display some interesting features. Three of the tombs had an associated mudbrick boat burial on their north side (see *Boats in Egyptian Funerary Religion*). One of these tombs also had an estate modelled in mud-covered rubble on its north side.

Another tomb had a tree plantation on its east side, the purpose of which was probably to provide cool shade for the *ba* of the deceased. A particularly fascinating feature was a raised platform with bulls' heads sitting on it, which ran around some of the mastabas. The heads were modelled out of mud but the horns were real, and it has been estimated that a tomb might be surrounded by up to three hundred of them. Throughout Egyptian history the bull was closely associated with kingship. The pharaoh was referred to as 'Mighty Bull', in the belief that he could assimilate the strength and virility of the animal.

Towards the end of the Early Dynastic Period, the mound-like superstructures of the mastabas at Saqqara were being constructed in the shape of a low stepped pyramid, and so it is possible to trace the development of the early royal tomb from the mastaba to the pyramid. By the Old Kingdom (c.2686 BC), the king was no longer buried in a mastaba, but his high officials continued to be buried in them. ◆

▼ *A recessed outer wall like a palace façade and bulls horns on a surrounding platform have been excavated at tomb 3504 at Saqqara.*

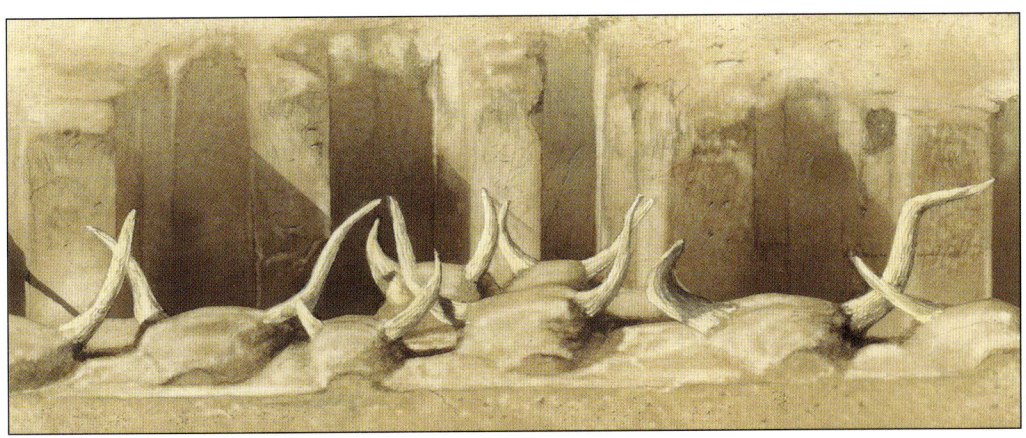

Pyramids

The word 'pyramid' (ancient Egyptian *mer*) comes from the Greek word *pyramis* meaning 'wheat cake' (presumably because such a cake resembled a pyramid in shape). The humble origin of the name belies the sheer magnificence of many of the ancient Egyptian pyramids, some of which, many would argue, are the most stupendous structures ever built.

Djoser's Step Pyramid

The earliest pyramid was not quite the type we usually picture, but rather a large stepped structure – hence its name, the Step Pyramid. It was built at Saqqara to house the burial of the Third-Dynasty king, Djoser (c.2667–c.2648 BC), and it is the earliest known monumental stone building. The idea of a stepped superstructure for a tomb was not new, (see *Mastabas*), but much about the Step Pyramid and its surrounding complex of courts, temples and other buildings was truly innovative.

The later Pyramid Texts emphasized the ascent of the dead king to the heavens, so perhaps the concept behind the Step Pyramid was to provide a giant ladder for the king to reach his heavenly destination. It has also been suggested that the pyramid might have represented the primordial mound that was believed to have risen out of the waters of chaos at the time of creation (an image also closely associated with the solar deity). Djoser's pyramid was the masterpiece of his great vizier and architect, Imhotep. The structure developed in stages. It began as an almost square mastaba tomb; it was then extended on all four sides; next a four-stepped pyramid was added over this structure; and finally it was converted into a six-stepped pyramid. It was built out of local

limestone and cased in the better quality Tura limestone from the quarries across the river. The shaft to the burial chamber beneath the pyramid was plugged with a granite boulder weighing three tons.

The architects and builders of the time were experimenters – they made use of smaller and more easily portable stone blocks than were used in the later pyramids. The columns they built were engaged rather than free-standing, and they were built up from segments of stone rather than being carved from single blocks. The builders worked the stone in a way that imitated earlier, more organic building materials. The ceiling blocks and columns in the processional way, for example, were carved to look like bundles of reeds. If the tomb itself imitated a ladder to the Afterlife, perhaps the entrance colonnade was designed to symbolize the Field of Reeds – the place of purification for both the sun and the dead king.

▲ *Djoser's Step Pyramid complex at Saqqara measures over 500 x 250m (547 x 273yd).*

The Meidum Pyramid

The next great achievement in the development of tomb building was the pyramid at Meidum. This was the earliest occurrence of a stepped pyramid with the steps filled in and cased to form a smooth-sided, geometrically true pyramid. The monument may well have been begun by Huni (c.2637–c.2613 BC), the last ruler of the Third Dynasty, and it was completed by Sneferu (c.2613–c.2589 BC), the first ruler of the Fourth Dynasty. It began life as a seven-stepped pyramid, which was cased in Tura limestone. It was later enlarged to become an eight-stepped structure and the steps were cased again. Finally the steps were filled in and cased a final time. It is possible that the smooth sides of the pyramid were thought to symbolize the rays of the sun.

▶ *Today the pyramid at Meidum stands as a three-step tower rising from a mound of debris, probably the result of collapse and quarrying.*

◀ *The pyramids at Giza are one of the seven wonders of the ancient world.*

Khufu's Great Pyramid

The pyramid was an icon of the cult of the sun god Re, which increased in importance during the Fourth Dynasty (c.2613–c.2494 BC). It was the most magnificent of status symbols – an unmistakable expression of the might of kingship and the success of the particular ruler buried in it. The most enormous of these structures was the Great Pyramid of the Fourth-Dynasty king Khufu (c.2589–c.2566 BC), built on the desert plateau at Giza. Its complete height would originally have been 146m (479ft). One of its greatest architectural features and feats of engineering is the 'Grand Gallery', which leads to the burial chamber. This is 46m (150ft) long and over 8m (26ft) high, with a huge corbelled vault constructed with its

▼ *The 'Bent Pyramid' at Dahshur was built, together with the neighbouring 'Red Pyramid' by King Sneferu.*

roofing slabs laid at an angle steeper than the slope of the gallery, in order to prevent a build-up of pressure at any one point. Similar precautions were taken in the granite burial chamber, where five compartments were built above the flat ceiling to minimize any risk of collapse.

The sun and the stars

The construction of the pyramids shows that the ancient Egyptians were incredibly successful engineers. They were also very much concerned with the rituals and beliefs surrounding death. It is clear from the Pyramid Texts that there was a fundamental solar element to their funerary religion, but there was also an important stellar one. In the Great Pyramid, two shafts running from the burial chamber were aligned with various stars, including the constellation of Orion (divinely personified by the Egyptians as the god Sah). Orion was possibly intended as the destination of

the king's *ba* when he ascended to take his place among the circumpolar stars. In this and similar ways the ancient Egyptians incorporated the stars into their religious beliefs as well as using a certain amount of astronomical observation in the building of the pyramids, especially in the precise alignment of the tomb with the four cardinal points.

It was not until the reign of King Unas (c.2375–c.2345 BC) at the end of the Fifth Dynasty that the ancient Egyptians began to inscribe funerary texts on the interior walls of their kings' pyramids (see *Pyramid Texts*). From these we can begin to get a clearer idea of how the ancient Egyptians envisaged the rebirth of the king and his survival in the Afterlife. Rulers continued to be buried in pyramids right up until the Second Intermediate Period (c.1650–c.1550 BC). After this, Thebes became the royal burial site, where tombs were cut into the desert cliffs. Meanwhile, non-royals could choose to incorporate a small mudbrick or stone model of a pyramid, known as a pyramidion, into the design of their tombs. This ties in with the notion of the democratization of funerary religion. ◆

Benben Stones and Obelisks

Each of the pyramids would originally have sported a gilded pyramidion (a mini-pyramid) at its pinnacle, which would have glinted strikingly in the sunlight. This feature, together with the sloping sides of the entire structure resembling the rays of the sun as they are seen to jut through the clouds, would have made the pyramid an appropriate icon of solar religion. This was also an important aspect of funerary religion, especially of the king, and especially during the Old Kingdom (c.2686–c.2181 BC).

The sun cult at Heliopolis
The heyday of the pyramid was during the Old Kingdom, a time when the cult of the sun god Re at Heliopolis rose to the forefront of Egyptian state religion, and one of the king's five names came to be introduced by the title 'Son of Re'. The prototype for the true pyramid may well have been the focal point of the cult at Heliopolis. This was a squat standing stone, pointed at its apex, known as a *benben* (from the verb *weben*, 'to rise', which also provides the origins of the ancient Egyptian word for the cap-stone or pyramidion at the top of a pyramid – a *benbenet*). This monument, the original and most sacred of the *benbens*, was erected at Heliopolis at least as early as the First Dynasty. It may well have symbolized the primordial mound that appeared out of the watery chaos of Nun, whence the sun rose for the first time and creation began. It was certainly believed to have been the first point hit by the rays of the rising sun. It is also possible that this stone symbolized the petrified semen of Atum, the creator god of Heliopolis, whose act of masturbation played a key role in the creation of the divine personifications of air and moisture, Shu and Tefnut.

During the Fifth Dynasty, the structure was imitated in sun temples, which were associated with royal pyramid burials, but were also clearly dedicated to the sun god Re. The sun temple of Niuserre

▼ *The obelisks of Tuthmosis I and Hatshepsut at Karnak temple. There is a description of the quarrying and transport of two granite obelisks to Karnak on the walls of Hatshepsut's mortuary temple at Deir el-Bahri.*

◄ *This obelisk from Luxor Temple was erected in the Place de la Concorde in Paris in 1836 using ropes and pulleys.*

(c.2445–c.2421 BC) at Abu Gurab, north of Abusir (part of the necropolis of the ancient capital at Memphis), was named 'Delight of Re'. It would originally have been dominated by an enormous limestone *benben*, 36m (118ft) in height.

▼ *If the 'unfinished obelisk' in the Aswan granite quarries had been successfully removed from the rock it would have been 42m (138ft) tall and weighed 1197 tons.*

This sacred stone would have stood on a pedestal in the form of a limestone truncated pyramid, 20m (66ft) high, with red granite around the base.

Gold-tipped obelisks

Throughout history, the ancient Egyptians also incorporated a more tapering, needle-like version of the *benben* into the design of their tombs and temple complexes. Today we call

these sacred stones obelisks. The ancient Egyptians called them *tekhen*, a word that might also relate to the verb *weben*. They too would originally have had gilded tips, which were also referred to as *benbenet*, and would have reflected the sun's rays majestically. The solar imagery was often extended to the designs carved on the obelisks, such as figures of baboons. These animals were observed to greet the rising sun with great excitement each morning, and to sit on their hind legs, their front paws raised at dawn in order to warm their undersides (hence the ancient Egyptian posture for worship and adoration). The splendour and elegance of the obelisk has continued to command respect, not only in Egypt but throughout the world, and obelisks have been removed from Egypt and re-erected in cities such as Rome, Paris, London and New York. ◆

The *benu*

Like the Greek phoenix, the Egyptian *benu*-bird was connected with the sun and rebirth. As a sacred bird of Heliopolis, the benu was closely associated with the solar deities Re and Atum, and with the obelisk and *benben* stone.

In the Pyramid Texts, the *benu*-bird appears as a yellow wagtail, but by the advent of the Book of the Dead, it was being represented as a kind of grey heron with a long, straight beak, and a two-feathered crest.

Chapter 83 of the Book of the Dead was the 'spell for being transformed into a *benu*-bird'.

The Great Sphinx

When we speak of the Sphinx, we are referring to the earliest colossal statue in Egypt. It is 73m (240ft) long, with a maximum height of 20m (66ft), and is probably a statue of the Fourth-Dynasty king Khafre (c.2558–c.2532 BC). His head, wearing a pleated linen *nemes*-headdress and a *uraeus*, is superimposed on the body of a lion – an animal closely associated with kingship due to its great power and might. In connection with the solar iconography of the pyramid, benben stone and obelisk, the lion was also regarded as a solar symbol in ancient Near Eastern cultures.

The word 'sphinx' comes from the Greek and means 'the strangler', but this implies that the statue had a terrifying aspect, and this was not an idea shared by the ancient Egyptians. It is possible that 'sphinx' was a distortion of the Egyptian *shesep ankh*, meaning 'living image'. Vast numbers of considerably smaller sphinxes have also survived from ancient Egypt. These include not only statues of rulers in sphinx form, but also gods, such as the avenue of ram-headed sphinxes (manifestations of the god Amun) that run between Karnak and Luxor temples.

Khafre's temples

The Sphinx was carved out of a natural outcrop of the limestone rock alongside Khafre's valley temple at Giza. The valley temple was the king's funerary temple, built on a quay at the edge of the Nile Valley and linked by means of a causeway to the smaller mortuary temple adjoining the eastern face of the pyramid. It is possible that the sphinx was intended to serve as a guardian for Khafre's splendid valley temple. But there was another temple, more closely associated with the great statue, located beneath its front paws. Referred to as the Sphinx temple, it appears to have been specifically dedicated to the

Sphinx. It is impossible to be certain about the architectural symbolism and functioning of this temple, because no Old Kingdom texts have survived that refer to it, and none of the Old Kingdom

▲ *The head of the Sphinx was carved from a much better building stone than the soft layers of the body, which have been severely eroded, while the base is carved from a petrified hard shoal and coral reef.*

the Dream Stela. It recounts the tale of Tuthmosis as a young prince on a hunting expedition at Giza. He fell asleep under the Sphinx and, as he slept, the Sphinx, as the solar and creator deity Khepri-Re-Atum, appeared to him in a dream. He promised Tuthmosis the throne of Egypt if he would repair the giant body of the statue and clear the windswept sand that had accumulated up to its neck. Tuthmosis did just this – he restored the lion body with stone cladding and built an open-air chapel between the paws of the Sphinx, with the stela as its centrepiece. ◆

▲ *Several New Kingdom stelae commemorating visits made to the restored Sphinx show a royal statue behind the Dream Stela.*

tombs at Giza belonged to priests or priestesses of its cult. Much about the temple remains a mystery, but it does seem that there was an important solar element to it. It has been suggested that its eastern and western sanctuaries were associated with the rising and setting sun, and that the Sphinx symbolized Khafre in the role of making offerings to the sun god in the court of the temple. However, it is also possible that the Sphinx was originally viewed as an image of the sun god himself, because this certainly appears to have been the case over 1,000 years later during the New Kingdom (c.1550– c.1069 BC), when the Sphinx came to be known as Horemakhet, or 'Horus-in-the-Horizon'.

Tuthmosis IV's dream

The Eighteenth-Dynasty king Tuthmosis IV (c.1400–c.1390 BC) was instrumental in restoring the Sphinx and reactivating its cult. He erected a granite stela, weighing 15 tons and 3.6m (12ft) high, made out of a lintel from one of the doorways of Khafre's mortuary temple, between the paws of the Sphinx. The upper part of this stela depicts the king making offerings to the Sphinx, which the hieroglyphs identify as Horus-in-the-Horizon.

It is because of its detailed inscription that the stela has come to be known as

▶ *The head of a king on the body of a lion, this bronze example depicting Tuthmosis III, was the most common type of sphinx, but sometimes they were ram-headed (criosphinxes) or hawk-headed (hierakosphinxes). 18th Dynasty.*

Boats in Egyptian Funerary Religion

◄ *Khufu's boat is 43m (142ft) long and 6m (19ft) wide; it has a maximum draft of 1.5m (5ft) and a displacement of 45 tons.*

been found in each. The boats were obviously intended to be dismantled because the pits are not large enough to have contained them when assembled. One of them has been pieced together and is on display in a specially built museum near the pyramid. Its 1,224 individual pieces were painstakingly 'stitched' together using vegetable fibre rope, and joined using mortise and tenon joints, to bring to life a breathtaking vessel measuring a magnificent 43m (142ft) long. Its prow and stern are in the form of papyrus stalks, and its design is based on that of a papyrus reed boat. The boat in the other pit has been photographed using a tiny camera inserted through a hole into the pit, but it has not yet been excavated.

Why boat pits?

Because the River Nile was the main thoroughfare through Egypt, boats were essential in Egyptian daily life. They were the only means of transport across the river, and were by far the most sensible means of travelling up and down the country. For this reason, it is not surprising that the boat should be so highly valued and that it was incorporated into the rituals of death and beliefs concerning the Afterlife.

There are several possible reasons for the occurrence of boat-shaped pits and buried boats in the vicinity of the Great Pyramid. The boatless pits must have been purely symbolic, and were presumably connected with the journeying of the king to the heavens after his death. It was believed that he needed to join the circumpolar stars in the northern sky, but he was also thought to voyage with the sun, and according to much mythology the sun god Re passed through the solar cycle

Boat-shaped pits have been excavated alongside royal mastaba and pyramid burials of the Early Dynastic Period and Old Kingdom (c.3100–c.2181 BC), but the most impressive are those associated with the Great Pyramid of Khufu at Giza. Close to the mortuary temple and three subsidiary pyramids just to the east of the Great Pyramid, five boat-shaped

pits were found that appear never to have actually housed boats, and were in fact symbolic.

However, just to the south of the pyramid, two more interesting pits were discovered. They are long, narrow and rectangular, but unlike the boat-shaped pits, they were actually intended for the burial of boats. Indeed, the disassembled parts of a real cedar-wood boat have

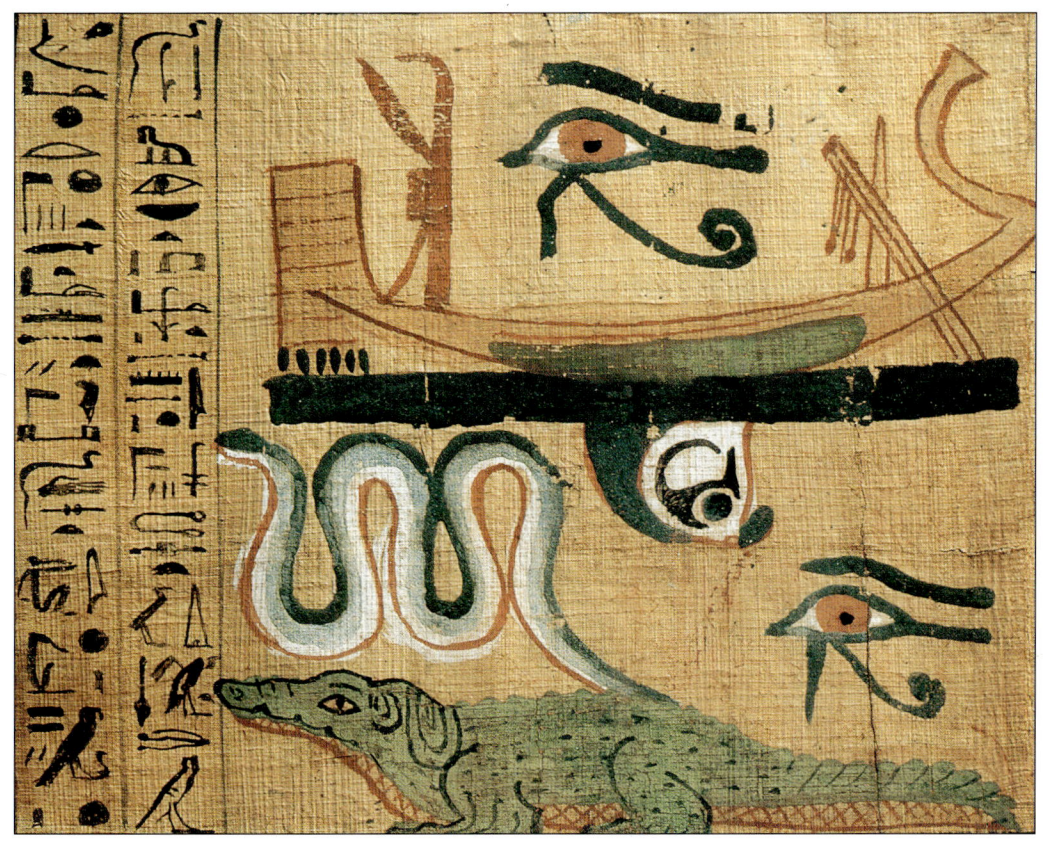

▲ The hieroglyph for 'follower' (shemset) – a crook or staff with a knife and some sort of package lashed to it – is often depicted in representations of the solar barque, such as this one from the Book of the Dead of Heruben. 21st Dynasty.

▲ A boat pit to the south of the mortuary temple on the east face of Djedefre's pyramid at Abu Roash, recalls the one just outside the entrance to Khufu's temple alongside the Great Pyramid.

by boat. A boat pit might also have been deemed necessary to symbolize the transportation of the king's *ka* statue.

The significance of the real boats is likely to have been somewhat different. The fact that they were deliberately dismantled when they could have been buried whole, and the fact that their

burials would have lain just outside the original enclosure wall of the pyramid complex, indicates that they are less likely to have had a symbolic role in the funerary complex. They were probably used in the funeral cortege of the dead king, and having performed their function, they were ritually disposed of close to the royal burial.

Model boats

Throughout Egyptian history boats were depicted on the walls of non-royal tombs, and during the Middle Kingdom (c.2055–c.1650 BC) it was popular to place wooden models of them

in the tombs. Because the ancient Egyptians travelled by boat while alive, they expected to do so in the Afterlife. An actual journey that might be depicted in painted or model form was the transport of the dead body from the realm of the living on the east bank to that of the dead on the west bank. A symbolic journey that might also have been represented was the pilgrimage made by the deceased to the cult centre and legendary burial place of Osiris at Abydos. ◆

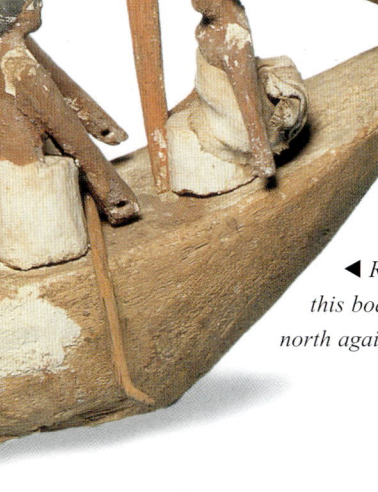

◀ Relying on oars and the current, this boat would have been heading north against the wind.

Rock-cut Tombs

Throughout Egyptian history, tombs were cut into the desert rock. Both mastabas and pyramids often had subterranean burial chambers excavated into the rock, but the term 'rock-cut tomb' tends to be used to describe a tomb that has been cut into the desert cliffs, with no superstructure, but very often with a separate funerary chapel or temple.

The best-known rock-cut tombs in Egypt are those located in the area known as the Valley of the Kings, on the west bank of the Nile at Thebes (modern Luxor). It is home to undoubtedly the most famous of the tombs, that of the Eighteenth-Dynasty king Tutankhamun (c.1336–c.1327 BC), which was discovered by the British archaeologist Howard Carter in 1922. The world continues to marvel at the treasure it yielded. Tutankhamun was actually a relatively minor ruler of the New Kingdom (c.1550–c.1069 BC) but, together with the Twenty-first and Twenty-second Dynasty burials excavated at Tanis by the French archaeologist Pierre Montet in 1939, his tomb was by far the best preserved of any royal tomb.

Contrary to popular belief, Tutankhamun's tomb was not intact on discovery – it had been entered, partly robbed, and resealed in antiquity – but the quality and quantity of the funerary equipment found in it were quite stupendous. Many of the objects are made of gold, lapis lazuli, turquoise, amethyst and other precious materials. They include wonderful examples of ancient Egyptian craftsmanship, such as Tutankhamun's mummy mask, coffins, jewellery and shrines, which are now on display in the Egyptian Museum, Cairo.

Despite the richness of its contents, Tutankhamun's tomb was far less grand than others in the Valley of the Kings. It consisted of only four small rooms rather than the usual long corridor-style

▲ *There are 62 tombs in the Valley of the Kings, the most famous being that of the young king Tutankhamun.*

▼ *This was the view of the antechamber of Tutankhamun's tomb that greeted Howard Carter when he first looked into it in 1922.*

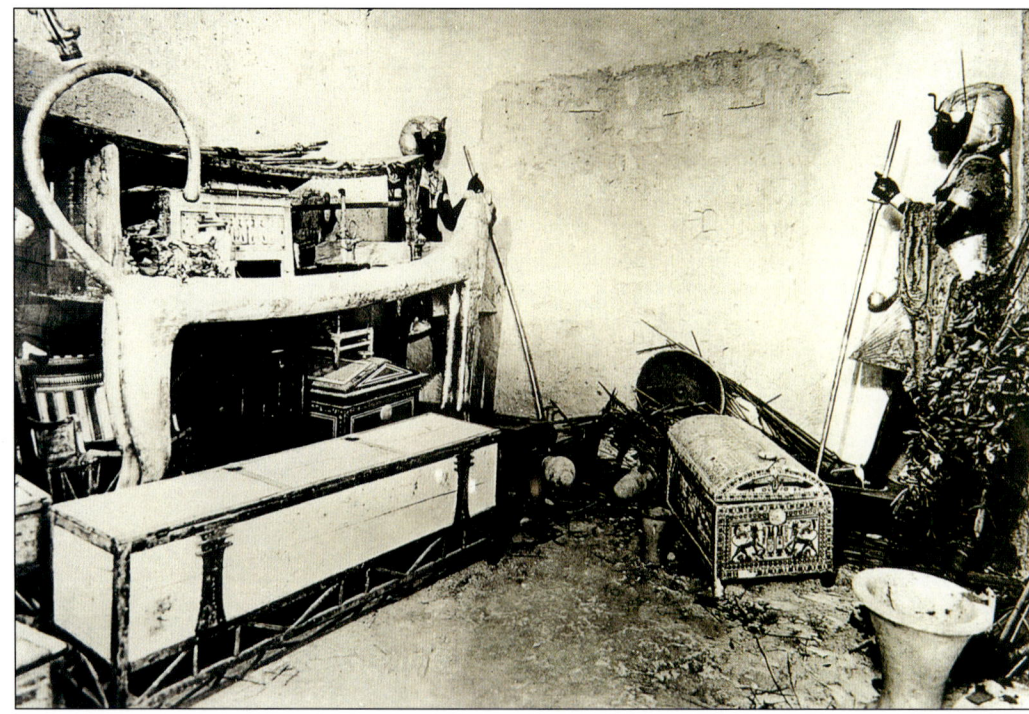

tomb, and as such was probably originally intended as a private burial place (perhaps that of his vizier Ay). On Tutankhamun's death, this tomb may have been hastily enlarged to receive a royal burial, but only one of the rooms was ever decorated.

Design features of the tombs

The first king to choose to have his tomb cut in the Valley of the Kings was probably Tuthmosis I (c.1504–c.1492 BC), the third ruler of the Eighteenth Dynasty. The character of the rock is likely to have dictated the somewhat meandering approach corridor to his squarish burial chamber. The tomb of his successor, Tuthmosis II (c.1492–c.1479 BC), appears to have been more carefully planned. It introduced two interesting new features – a bent axis to the approach corridor and an oval burial chamber. The sudden sharp left turn to the corridor may well have been devised to fool any prospective tomb robbers into believing that the blocked corridor continued straight onwards when in fact, behind another blocked wall, it headed off at a right angle. The oval burial chamber reminds us of the cartouche

▼ *The four canopic coffins containing Tutankhamun's internal organs are miniature replicas of the second of the king's three coffins.*

▶ *The lotiform chalice found in Tutankhamun's tomb is carved of a single piece of calcite and inlaid with blue pigment.*

used to surround the king's name, and in a similar way the walls of the chamber would have surrounded and protected the dead body of the king.

Tomb robbery and flooding

The ancient Egyptians had obviously learned by experience that the burial chambers needed to be safeguarded against both robbery and flooding. The unique survival of Tutankhamun's tomb reveals the lack of success the Egyptians had in protecting their dead and the material buried with them. The plunder of tombs continues to be a problem to the present day, as does the disastrous effect caused by occasional torrential rain that results in destructive flash floods racing through desert wadis such as the Valley of the Kings.

Tuthmosis III's architects introduced a deep 'well' into his tomb, perhaps to protect it against flooding or robbers. They also built a pillared antechamber between the well and the burial chamber, and four small rooms were cut into the two long sides of the burial chamber for the storage of funerary equipment.

Innovation also crept into the

tomb of Amenhotep II (c.1427–c.1400 BC), which had a rectangular, columned burial chamber with a sunken crypt at the far end. Horemheb's reign (c.1323–c.1295 BC) heralded the use of a tomb with a straight axis. Unique to the tomb of the Nineteenth-Dynasty king Seti I (c.1294–c.1279 BC) was a passage more than 136m (149yd) long below the burial chamber. Its end cannot be reached, but it seems to be approaching the level of the water table, and the idea behind it might have been the linking of the burial chamber to the primordial waters of creation. The last tomb to be cut in the Valley of the Kings was that of the last ruler of the New Kingdom, Ramesses XI, who died c.1069 BC.

Wall decoration

Like most rock-cut tombs throughout Egypt belonging to men of high status from viziers to craftsmen, the tombs in the Valley of the Kings were elaborately decorated. The walls of the royal rock-cut tombs were covered in paintings of detailed funerary scenes relating to the king's Afterlife, and his interaction with the gods and goddesses of the Egyptian pantheon. ◆

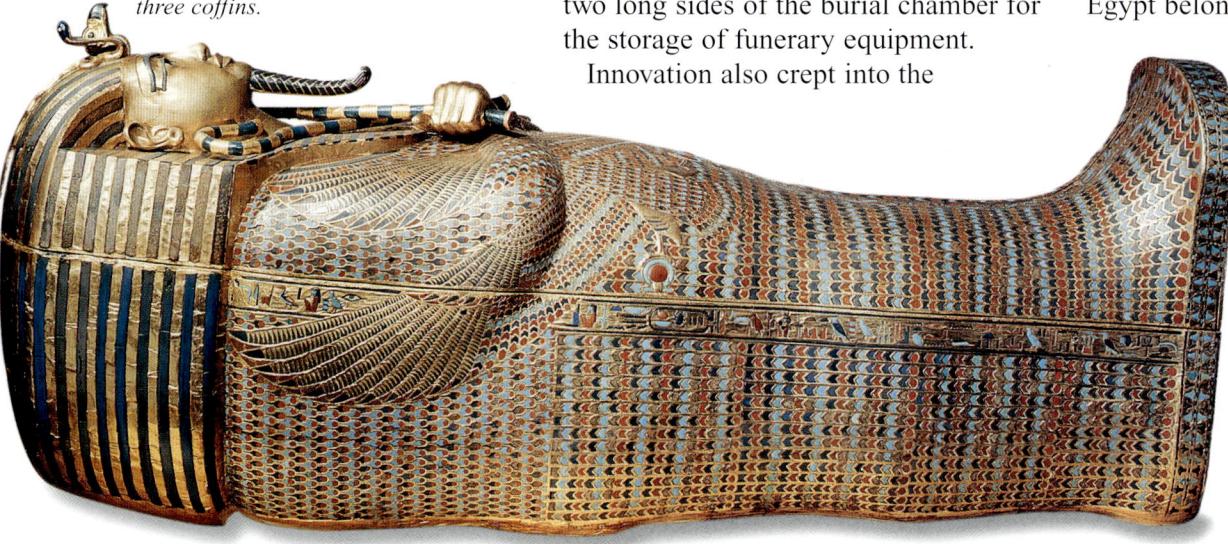

Tomb-builders' Towns and Villages

◄ The tools used by the tomb builders included copper and bronze chisels, adzes and spikes, heavy wooden mallets and hammers of hard stone bound into wooden hafts, and heavy wooden-handled bronze hoes.

storage bins and grain silos, has also been excavated in front of Menkaure's valley temple. This was a random arrangement of slum housing which eventually overtook the front of the valley temple.

The town of Kahun

The pyramid town of Kahun at Il-Lahun, at the eastern edge of the Faiyum some 100km (62 miles) south-east of Cairo, was specially built to house the men (and their families) who built the pyramid of the Twelfth-Dynasty king Senusret II (c.1880–c.1874 BC). It later provided homes for the priests, officials and their families who served the dead king's funerary cult. It was carefully planned and laid out on a grid system.

▼ Research into the genealogies of the builders at Deir el-Medina has shown that about 25 interrelated families lived in the village.

A great deal concerning the construction of the tombs of ancient Egypt, especially the pyramids, remains a mystery. But archaeologists have unearthed texts that refer to towns, and the towns that housed the tomb builders and craftsmen, or the priests, officials, guards and other personnel involved in the daily running of the funerary cults and complexes of the dead kings. The remains of such settlements have been discovered at Giza, Il-Lahun, Tell el-Amarna and Deir el-Medina on the Theban west bank.

The Giza settlements

At Giza, home to the magnificent Fourth-Dynasty pyramids of Khufu, Khafre and Menkaure, the names of two settlements are known. They are the southern Tjeniu ('boundary mark' or 'cultivation edge') of Khafre, which was probably to the south of the king's valley temple, and the northern Gerget ('settlement') of Khufu, which may have been situated around this king's valley temple. Mudbrick buildings, broken pottery, bread moulds, cooking pots,

animal bones, grinding stones, charcoal and ash have all been discovered in this area. Unfortunately, the ancient settlement appears to extend beneath the modern, ever-growing city of Cairo and its sewers, so further excavation is just about impossible. A community of small mud huts, with

Altogether, 220 small houses have been excavated in the western and southern parts of the town. The north-eastern area was the site of nine or ten sizeable urban estates, each with a large house, garden and granary – presumably the occupants of these were the king's highest officials.

Deir el-Medina

The settlement site that has yielded more written and archaeological evidence of daily life than any other is Deir el-Medina. During the New Kingdom (c.1550–c.1069 BC) it was home to the workmen (and their families) who quarried and decorated the rock-cut tombs in the Valley of the Kings on the west bank at Thebes. The small village was specially planned and constructed to serve this purpose. It was situated in a sheltered spot in the desert, between the Ramesseum and Medinet Habu, with relatively easy access to the Valley of the Kings. We know that the original outer enclosure wall of the village was built during the reign of the early Eighteenth-Dynasty king Tuthmosis I (c.1504–c.1492 BC) (probably the first king to be buried in the Valley of the Kings) because his cartouche has been found stamped on some of the bricks. However, throughout the village's lifetime (that is, for the duration of the New Kingdom, while kings were being buried in tombs in the Valley of the Kings), its founding father and patron deity was considered to be Tuthmosis I's father Amenhotep I (c.1525–c.1504 BC). At the end of the Eighteenth Dynasty,

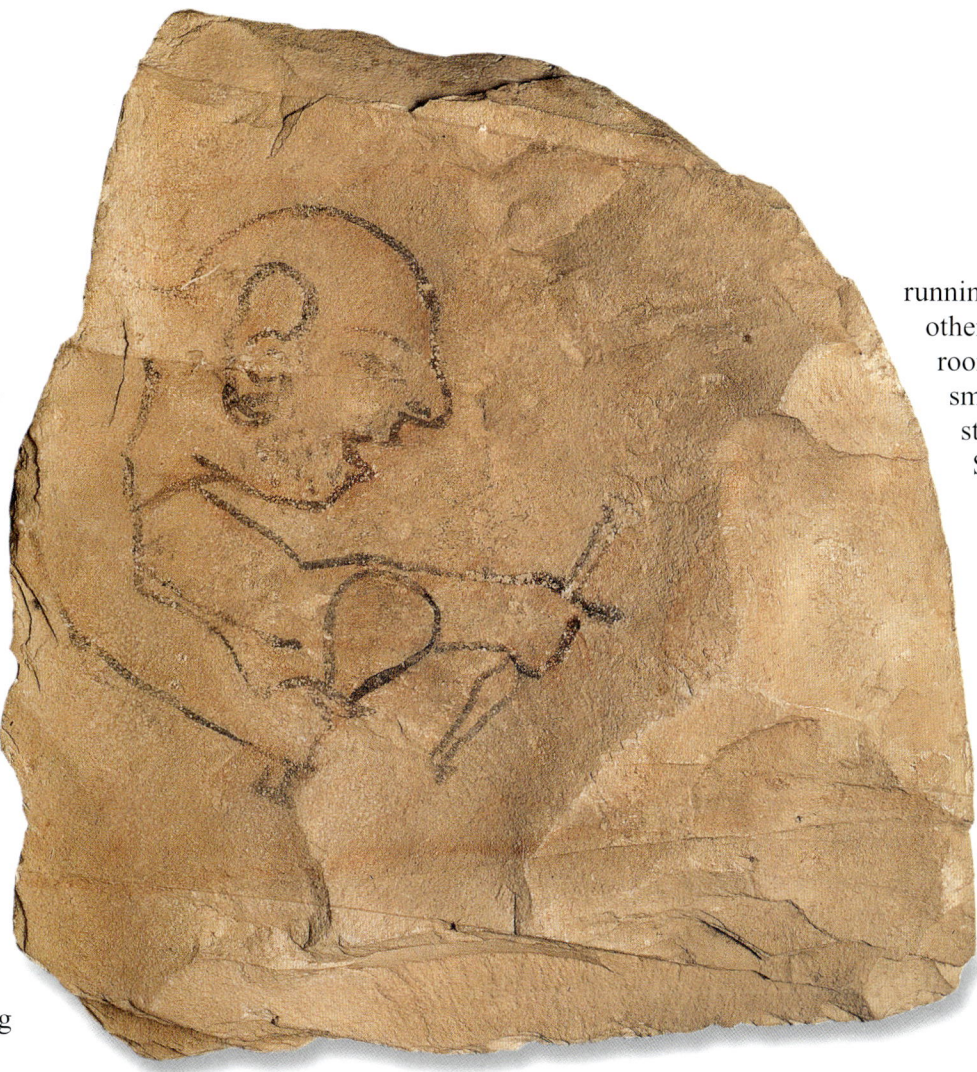

▲ *In addition to their work in the Valley of the Kings, the Deir el-Medina tomb builders such as this stonemason, might take commissions from the wealthy folk of Thebes to quarry and decorate their rock-cut tombs. 19th Dynasty.*

with the return to Thebes following the Amarna period (when the ruler Akhenaten overshadowed Thebes by building a new religious and political capital named Akhetaten in Middle Egypt), the village of Deir el-Medina was enlarged to include about 12 new houses.

The community was divided into an eastern and western section by a narrow street, which was probably originally roofed over. The 70 or so houses were all similar in design, built in a combination of the usual domestic building material, mudbrick, and rough limestone set in mortar. There were also certain architectural features of stone, such as doorways, and whitewashed walls to reflect the sun. The houses were 5–6m (16–20ft) wide, with four rooms running one behind the other, two large family rooms, followed by a smaller kitchen and storage room.

Staircases led to the flat roofs that served as extra living space, and cellars were often cut from the desert rock for cool storage. It has been suggested that at any one time the village housed about 25 interrelated families. Excavation beyond the confines of the village has revealed shrines – smaller versions of the huge stone temples of state deities such as Hathor – just to the north, stables for cows and donkeys, and a rubbish dump to the south. Most excitingly, on the desert hillside to the west, is the main cemetery, with beautifully decorated tombs of the village's inhabitants. There are tomb shafts, small mudbrick chapels, and miniature pyramids.

During the reign of Akhenaten (c.1352–c.1336 BC), the inhabitants of Deir el-Medina probably moved to the site today known as Tell el-Amarna in order to quarry out and decorate the tombs of the élite and royal family of the new city of Akhetaten. Here, in the desert about 1.2km (^{3}/4 mile) from the main city of Akhetaten, a village has been excavated. It was roughly 70m (77yd) square, with a thick enclosure wall surrounding 73 identically sized houses and one larger one. The whole settlement was divided into two unequal parts by a thick wall. In its environs were buildings such as chapels, pigsties and storehouses. ◆

Tomb Robbery

◀ *Upon death the king was identified with Osiris. Ramesses II's presence in his mortuary temple, the Ramesseum, includes semi-mummiform figures of him as Osiris attached to the columns.*

external threats (especially from the Libyans to the west and the Nubians to the south). Compared with these, tomb robbery might have been regarded as a minor trouble, but in fact it was taken extremely seriously. After all, to enter a sealed tomb and remove its contents, destroying – or at least endangering – the mummified body in the process (robbers often burned mummies) would have been considered a threat to the existence of the deceased in the Afterlife. In the case of the king it was even a threat to the stability and well-being of Egypt and its people, since the ancient Egyptians believed that the dead were able to affect the lives of the living.

T he plunder of Egyptian tombs is by no means a modern phenomenon. At all periods of ancient Egyptian history the possible threat of tomb robbery had to be guarded against, and precautions – such as stone portcullises, confusing corridors and deep pits – were incorporated into all types of tombs. The prolific ancient evidence for disturbance, destruction and theft from tombs reveals just how unsuccessful these measures tended to be. Of most interest to tomb robbers were goods that could be disposed of easily, such as textiles, perfumes and cosmetics, precious woods and ivory. Also valued were objects made from materials that could be recycled, such as gold and silver.

The most detailed and extensive documentation about tomb (and temple) robbery dates to the end of the New Kingdom, during the reigns of Ramesses IX (c.1126–c.1108 BC) and Ramesses XI (c.1099–c.1069 BC). This was a time of various problems, such as ineffectual

rulers, corruption and bribery throughout officialdom, a possible civil war, agricultural failure, inflation and

▼ *In this illustration from Olfert Dapper's* Description de l'Afrique *(1686) the tomb robbers are huddled around an Egyptian mummy.*

▲ *The hypostyle hall at Medinet Habu provided a barrier between the outer courts of the mortuary temple and the mysterious inner sanctuaries.*

The tomb robbery papyri

A number of judicial papyri, known as the 'tomb robbery papyri', tell us how the tomb robbers were dealt with. As they concerned the plunder of royal tombs in the Valley of the Kings, it is not surprising that the king seems to have been personally responsible for setting up a commission to investigate the robberies. A court (*kenbet*) was set up to hear the proceedings at Ramesses III's mortuary temple at Medinet Habu,

and scribes were present at all times to record the trials and the confessions. The court records appear to have been hidden for safekeeping in the mortuary temple of Medinet Habu.

The document known as Papyrus Mayer B of Ramesses IX's reign is a detailed account of the theft of bronze and copper vessels, utensils, clothes and textiles from the tomb of Ramesses IX in the Valley of the Kings. Other documents contain references to the theft of objects by the foreman Paneb from the tomb of Seti II, and an attempted entry into the tomb of Ramesses II and his children's tomb in

the twenty-ninth year of Ramesses III's reign. (This is the same year as the earliest strike in recorded history, staged by the workman of Deir el-Medina when they did not receive their usual pay.)

The Abbott and Amherst Papyri are dated to the sixteenth year of Ramesses IX's reign. They recount the inspection of both royal and non-royal tombs that it was claimed had been violated, and the beatings and confessions of certain thieves. Other papyri contain accounts of thefts by priests from temple buildings (including Ramesses III's temple at Medinet Habu), and the recovery of gold, silver and copper from tomb thieves, all of whom turned out to be members of the necropolis staff.

Punishment for theft

There is evidence of the guilty being imprisoned in the Temple of Maat at Thebes, threats of mutilation, including having the nose and ears cut off, and of being sent to Ethiopia. But the ultimate punishment for tomb robbery must have been death. Seven men were put to death on the stake following a trial described in three separate papyri. ◆

Royal mummy caches

The tomb robberies in the Valley of the Kings at the end of the New Kingdom seriously threatened the survival of the royal mummies. In about 1000 BC the worried priests made the important decision to transfer the bodies of 56 dead kings and queens to safer hiding places. Forty of these mummies were discovered in a tomb near Deir el-Bahri in 1881. The other 16 were unearthed 17 years later in the tomb of Amenhotep II in the Valley of the Kings.

Popular Religion

Ancient Egyptian life was beset by trials and tribulations. These included dangerous animals such as scorpions, snakes, hippopotami, crocodiles, lions and hyenas; the loss of livestock and crops; famine; infertility; infant mortality and illness. All these had to be contended with, and religious beliefs were often the best way to explain otherwise inexplicable calamities. Rituals could help to solve everyday problems and maintain stability and well being.

'Popular religion' is the term used to describe this day-to-day religion of the people, but the evidence is so biased towards the literate, wealthy minority that it requires careful detective work to glean any information about the ideas and practices of the ordinary person. We can, however, learn about the private aspects of folk religion from finds such as a desperate, childless woman's votive offering of a fertility figurine at the local shrine of Hathor, the cow goddess of fertility; and the more public ones, such as a community's celebration of a divine festival at the local cult temple.

Magic and superstition played a crucial part in daily life, and were by no means considered unorthodox or an alternative to the religion of the state temples. A priest used to performing rituals in the cult of a state deity could also be called upon to carry out what we would term magic or sorcery. State and popular religion were clearly interrelated.

◀ *Crocodiles and hippopotami were among the perils of daily life that needed to be safeguarded against. This Nilotic scene appears on the wall of Meremka's 6th dynasty tomb at Saqqara.*

Magic

Clement of Alexandria, writing in the third century AD, observed that 'Egypt was the mother of magicians', and right up to the present day, Egypt has been viewed by those outside it as a place of magic and mysticism. The ancient Egyptians had a word, *heka*, which we translate as 'magic'. But we must not corrupt its meaning with the modern associations of magic – the idea of magic as non-establishment, or as an alternative to the generally accepted religious norm, would not have applied in ancient Egypt.

Heka, for the ancient Egyptians, conveyed a sense of the catalyst or energy that made creation possible. So every time a ritual was performed involving *heka*, it was as if a further development was thought to have been made in the process of creation. In the mythology of creation, *heka* was associated with *sia*, 'divine knowledge', and *hu*, 'divine utterance'. *Heka* itself was considered to be neither good or bad, but as an energy or power it could be channelled in either direction. The recorded incidents of what might be called antisocial magic in ancient Egypt tend to be fairly rare before the Roman Period, and any instances of unacceptable magic were usually attributed to foreign sorcerers. Similar to *heka* was *akhu*, which tends to be translated as 'sorcery', 'enchantments' or 'spells'. Again, *akhu* was in itself neither a negative nor a positive phenomenon and it could be worked in either direction.

There would have been certain members of each local community

◀ *Seneb, an achondroplastic dwarf, was Chief of all Palace Dwarves, in charge of the royal wardrobe and a priest of the mortuary cults of kings Khufu and Djedefre, so he was clearly highly respected and by no means ostracized.*

Magical cures

Magic aided the search for an answer to the perennial question 'Why me?' If a woman was suffering from a headache and convulsions, she might be visited by a respected member of the community (see *Who Performed Magic?*). He or she might trace the source of the disease to the anger of a particular deity, the magic of a foreign sorcerer, the malevolence of a demon or the ghost of a dead relative (see *The Negative Influence of the Dead*). The solution might then have been the performance of a ritual, including the recitation of a spell, in order to cure the woman. Deities and the dead tended to cause particular problems for the living when their temples or funerary chapels fell into disrepair or their offerings were forgotten.

who were credited with the ability to perform rituals using *heka*. There were also people who were believed to have an intrinsic possession of the force – either having been born with it, as dwarves were thought to be, or gaining it during certain periods of their life, as was the case with breast-feeding women. All kings, deities and the dead, by their very nature, were thought to have a certain degree of *heka*.

God of magic

The ancient Egyptians chose to personify divinely all that was crucial to them, including abstract concepts and natural phenomena. In this way they could pay their respects and make offerings to them, in order to ensure their continued and benevolent existence. The magical force of *heka* was divinely personified as the god Heka, who was represented in human form, holding snakes crossed in front of him. Like the household gods and goddesses, no major cult centres dedicated to Heka, or temples built in honour of him. He was worshipped as a secondary deity at Heliopolis, Memphis and Esna, and his

presence would have been ubiquitous in the temples throughout the country dedicated to other deities. We can discover something of the nature and characteristics of Heka by reading a range of ancient texts from different periods of Egyptian history. The Coffin Texts of the Middle Kingdom (c.2055–c.1650 BC) describe him as 'the unique lord made before duality had yet come into being', while he is referred to as 'Lord of Oracles, Lord of Miracles, who predicts what will happen' in an inscription found on the Graeco-Roman temple at Esna.

We also know of a goddess called Weret Hekau, meaning 'Great of Magic'. She took the form of a cobra, and it is possible that the snake-shaped wands used by those skilled in magic were crafted in this way in order to represent this goddess. The rearing cobra, known as a *uraeus*, on the front of the royal headdress, which was poised ready to spit venom at the king's enemies, was also sometimes described as *weret hekau*.

Wands and spells

A variety of wands and other paraphernalia of popular ritual have survived from ancient Egypt, as have collections of magic spells recorded on papyrus. The aim of these spells tended to be to ward off danger, such as the threats posed by snakes and scorpions, and to prevent or cure illness and particularly problems relating to fertility, pregnancy and birth. As in funerary religion, there was clearly a strongly held belief in the creative power of the words and images used in Egyptian magic. Knowledge of the relevant names was essential for the magic to prove effective.

Another important aspect of ancient Egyptian magic was sympathetic magic.

The mythology told that as a young boy, Horus had survived the threat of snakes and scorpions in the marshes of the Delta, and so if children were identified with the young god, they too could be protected from harm. Similarly, the goddess Isis (or Hathor, depending on the text) had successfully given birth to Horus, and so a woman having a difficult labour might transfer the pain by identifying herself with that goddess (see *Rites of Passage*). ◆

▲ *This wooden female figurine, found in a tomb under the Ramesseum in western Thebes, holds metal snake wands. It is uncertain whether the figure represents a goddess with a leonine head (perhaps Beset) or a woman wearing a mask.*

▲ *The deity Heka was represented anthropomorphically, sometimes holding two crossed snakes.*

Who Performed Magic?

Every community in Egypt must have had at least one wise person to whom the local people turned in times of need. This person was trusted and believed able to offer advice and perform rituals, using *heka*, or magic, to solve people's problems. Various titles have survived indicating the particular areas of expertise of these people. As was usual with Egyptian professions, it is likely that a father would have handed down his skills and secret knowledge to his son (or a mother to her daughter), and so one family would probably have become well known for practising magic over many generations.

Chiefs of mysteries

The word *hekau* (sometimes translated 'magician') existed as a general term for anyone who used magic, and a title that was obviously associated with magic was that of *Hery Seshta*, 'Chief of Mysteries or Secrets'. This title was found on the lid of a wooden box in a tomb of the late Middle Kingdom found under the Ramesseum in western Thebes. The box was among a selection of objects that had evidently been used for magical purposes. They included spells and religious papyri, a bronze snake wand, a wooden female figure wearing a mask of Beset (the female form of the protective spirit-deity Bes) and holding metal snake wands, a female fertility figurine, an ivory clapper and part of a magic rod.

The owner of this equipment for performing magical rituals was a priest, who would presumably have played an important role in the life of the local temple and that of the community. It may have been the figure known as the Lector Priest, whose job was also an extramural one. It was the Lector Priest who was responsible for reciting the spells in the temple, and during the embalming process and funerals. Among their other special skills, Lector

Priests were believed to be able to interpret dreams.

Other temple titles associated with the performance of magical rites were '*Hekau* of the House of Life' and 'Scribe of the House of Life'. There would have been a House of Life in most temple complexes. It was a place of copying, reading and research, rather like a library, scriptorium, school and university rolled into one.

Another important man was the *Sau*. It is uncertain exactly what he did, but the word *sa* is the word for both 'protection' and 'amulet', and so *Sau*

▲ *The lioness goddess Sekhmet, who was feared as the bringer of disease, paradoxically became associated with healing because of the need to appease her wrath. The title 'Priest of Sekhmet' became synonymous with 'doctor'.*

tends to be given the rather ambiguous translation, 'amulet man'. Perhaps he was responsible for making the amulets required by the local villagers or townspeople. Or perhaps, once a craftsman had manufactured the amulets, he was able to perform the ritual that would imbue the amulets with magical significance and supernatural

▲ *Selket appears as a protective deity together with Isis, Nephthys and Neith on the four corners of Tutankhamun's golden shrine.*

Warding off crocodiles

Boatmen on the River Nile faced the daily danger of attack by crocodiles. Sanctuaries of the crocodile god Sobek were erected at points on the river where these creatures congregated in the greatest numbers, but extra protection could be gained with the use of spells, amulets, wands and magic rods. Herdsmen protected their cattle against the threat of crocodiles by using a particular hand gesture and reciting spells for 'warding off the crocodile by the herdsmen'.

Scorpion charmers

Someone whose skills would have been much sought after was the *Kherep Selket*, literally, 'the one who has power over the scorpion goddess' – or, the local scorpion charmer (who no doubt also charmed snakes). The enormous numbers of spells to ward off snakes and scorpions, and to cure their bites, indicate the extent of the problem, and one that is still common in Egypt today. Modern snake charmers use practical techniques to ensnare their prey, but they also rely on magical chanting.

In ancient Egypt, a Lector Priest and a doctor could also hold the title *Kherep Selket*. The title *Sunu*, 'doctor' or 'physician', was held by people who prescribed both medical and magical remedies (see *Medicine*). The priests of the lioness goddess Sekhmet specialized in medicine and were closely associated with magic. Because this goddess was feared as the bringer of plague and other disease, magical rituals had to be performed in order to appease her and dissuade her from doing harm. ◆

powers. The records show that the *Sau* could be a woman, especially if she was also a midwife or a nurse.

A more specifically female title was *Rekhet* (literally 'knowing one'), which can probably best be translated 'wise woman'. The *Rekhet* appears to have been a medium, so if someone believed he was suffering because of the anger of one of his deceased relatives, he would consult a Rekhet. She would then liaise with the spirit world to find out which relative required appeasing (see *The Negative Influence of the Dead*).

▲ *Animal figurines (usually turtles, lions and crocodiles) were often attached to the top side of decorated hollow 'magic rods' which were probably used to establish the magician's authority over these various animals.*

Medicine

As far as the ancient Egyptians were concerned, there was no clear distinction between magic and medicine, and the two were fundamentally interrelated. About ten papyri have survived containing texts that today we call magico-medical texts because they combine the use of various remedies (to be taken internally, applied externally, or administered by fumigation), together with spells to be recited as part of magical rituals incorporating amulets and other such devices. It was crucial that the seemingly rational cures, which clearly influenced Greek medicine, were used in conjunction with spells. A woman suffering from irregular periods, for example, was advised to take a herbal remedy while reciting an incantation.

As already noted, the title *Sunu*, which means 'doctor' or 'physician', was held by people who practised both practical medical and magical techniques. The priests of the goddess Sekhmet would have been involved in temple rituals, but they also specialized in medicine.

Magico-medical papyri

During the third century AD, Clement of Alexandria observed that of the 42 books that comprised the sum total of all Egyptian knowledge, six were devoted to medicine, covering the topics of anatomy, illnesses, surgical instruments, drugs, eye ailments and gynaecology. These books have never been discovered, but various papyri do provide us with interesting information on all these subjects. Diagnosis was clearly based on both clinical examination and empirical knowledge. Pregnancy, for example, was diagnosed by pulse rate, propensity to vomit and internal gas, together with the appearance of the eyes, breasts and skin pigmentation. It appears that the Egyptian approach to medicine was perhaps more 'scientific' than in Babylonia and Assyria, where illness

tended to be more readily attributed to possession by demons. The ancient Egyptians accepted that some illnesses were incurable and so did not attempt to treat them. They also realized, for example, the effect of diet on a person's health (a Roman Period papyrus, Papyrus Insinger, blames ailments in the limbs on overeating).

▲ *This wooden statue represents a doctor who was practising his medical skills as early as the 5th Dynasty.*

Many of the ingredients for the prescriptions in the magico-medical texts are decidedly unappealing. For example, at least 19 different types of excrement are mentioned, including that

▶ *The medicinal use of onion appears frequently in the magico-medical papyri, for example in remedies for snake bites. This wall painting in the Theban tomb of Nakht shows them being carried. 18th Dynasty.*

of the fly and the ostrich. The logic behind such a peculiar choice of medicine appears to have been the principle of treating like with like. Rotting food trapped in the body was thought to cause a range of problems, and remedies containing faeces were thought to encourage these residues to travel out of the body.

Useful drugs

The Egyptians were the first people to use a number of drugs that modern studies have proved would have been medicinally effective. Honey, for example, was used both for magical and ritual purposes (see *Demons* and *Rites of Passage*), and for medical ones. It is now known to be resistant to bacterial growth, to act as a hypertonic – drawing water from bacterial cells, causing them to shrivel and die – and to exhibit antibiotic action due to a bacterial enzyme called inhibine which is secreted by the pharyngeal glands of the bee. It has proved to be efficacious against staphylococcus, salmonella and candida bacteria, and has been used to treat surgical wounds, ulcers and burns. In the Nineteenth-Dynasty Papyrus Leiden 1,348, the first of the spells prescribed for the cure of burns was to be said over a dressing of honey.

Onion occurs in the ancient texts, and it is now known that onion juice is an antibiotic, a diuretic and an expectorant.

▶ *Only the lower portion survives of this statue of the kneeling figure of the physician Horkheb. Beneath his offering of* hes-*jars is an inscribed 'Appeal to the Living' that priests should make offerings to his spirit now that he is dead, with a curse on those who fail to do so. 26th Dynasty.*

▲ *A number of implements are depicted on an offering table on this wall relief in the temple of Kom Ombo. There is much uncertainty as to their use, but they are probably Roman surgical instruments (the relief dates to the latter half of the 2nd century AD).*

Garlic was also used for medicinal purposes, and its healing properties are generally accepted today. It is said to contain an amino-acid derivative called allium, which releases the enzyme allinase. Its antibacterial qualities (it is an antibiotic exhibiting 1% of the strength of penicillin) are useful for treating wounds, and it is antifungal against candida. Thanks to the presence of methyl allyl trisulphide, which works to dilate the blood-vessel walls, it thins blood, lowers blood pressure and helps to prevent heart attack. It also lowers cholesterol levels, aids digestion and stimulates the immune system.

Ox liver or its juice was employed in ancient Egypt for night blindness, and we now know that animal liver is high in vitamin A and may indeed be effective against some forms of night blindness.

The various prescriptions did not necessarily have to be taken internally, but might be applied to parts of the body – for instance, raw meat used on wounds is very good for stopping bleeding. ◆

The mouse cure

Some outlandish remedies, which we would not expect to find anywhere but in ancient sources, do actually occur much closer to home and almost to the present day. For example, according to the Nineteenth-Dynasty papyrus now known as Berlin 3027, which deals with the illnesses of young children and their mothers, the cure for an uncertain illness called *sesmi* was to eat a cooked mouse. This remedy can be found used in a very similar way in the works of Dioscorides, Pliny, the Algerian physician 'Abd er-Razzak at the end of the seventh century AD, and the Arabic physician Ibn el-Betar in the thirteenth century AD. Mouse also figures in Culpeper's *Pharmacopoeia Londinensis* (1653), and in the *Pharmacopoeia Universalis* (1831). It has been said that in England during the 1920s, mouse was flayed, fried, boiled or made into pie and given to children in order to cure incontinence, dribbling and whooping cough.

Because it was usual for the ingestion of remedies to be accompanied by magic rites, Papyrus Berlin 3027 states that the bones of the mouse should be wrapped in a linen cloth (often stipulated for amuletic devices), knotted with seven knots (a magic number) and worn around the neck. A similar practice has been found among the Tlokwa of Botswana. The magical potency of the mouse may relate to a belief expressed by Pliny, and found in medieval bestiaries, that the mouse spontaneously emerged from the Nile mud after inundation.

Demons

The ancient Egyptians used magic to guard against the possible threat of demons and other malevolent forces, such as evil spirits, ghosts and hostile manifestations of deities. Demons were believed to be able to cause a variety of problems, especially illness. It has already been noted that the ancient Egyptians did not regard magic and medicine as distinct entities, but as very much interrelated (see *Medicine*). Demons were particularly associated with the goddess Sekhmet, who was regarded as the bringer of plague and other serious illness. In fact, there was a class of demon known as the 'Messengers of Sekhmet'. Sekhmet was also associated with fire and heat, so a fever might be blamed on her demons. Headaches and stomach problems were often said to be caused by demons contaminating the ill person's body, and so an emetic might be prescribed in an attempt to rid the person of the demon.

The desert and the netherworld

Demons were thought either to live in the desert, which was barren and associated with Seth, the god of chaos and infertility, or in an inverted netherworld. This meant that they lived upside down, so their mouths were where their anuses should have been, and they were said to eat their own faeces. In direct contrast to humans, for whom honey was sweet and delicious, demons were believed to find it bitter, and even to fear it. For this reason, honey was ideal for use in rituals to ward off demons and evil spirits. After giving birth, a woman might eat a cake made of honey, presumably to give her energy, but also to keep demons at bay at this particularly vulnerable time in her and her newborn baby's life. Garlic was also believed to have an apotropaic effect on demons. It was said to harm them, and so it was used in spells and rituals to protect young children against malevolent spirits. ◆

▲ *In ancient Egyptian religion the knife was considered a magic weapon.*

▼ *An important aim of funerary spells was to help the dead person deal with demons in the underworld. The donkey was identified with the demon par excellence, Seth: in the Book of the Dead of Chensumose, it is depicted trussed as a way of controlling its malevolence. 21st Dynasty.*

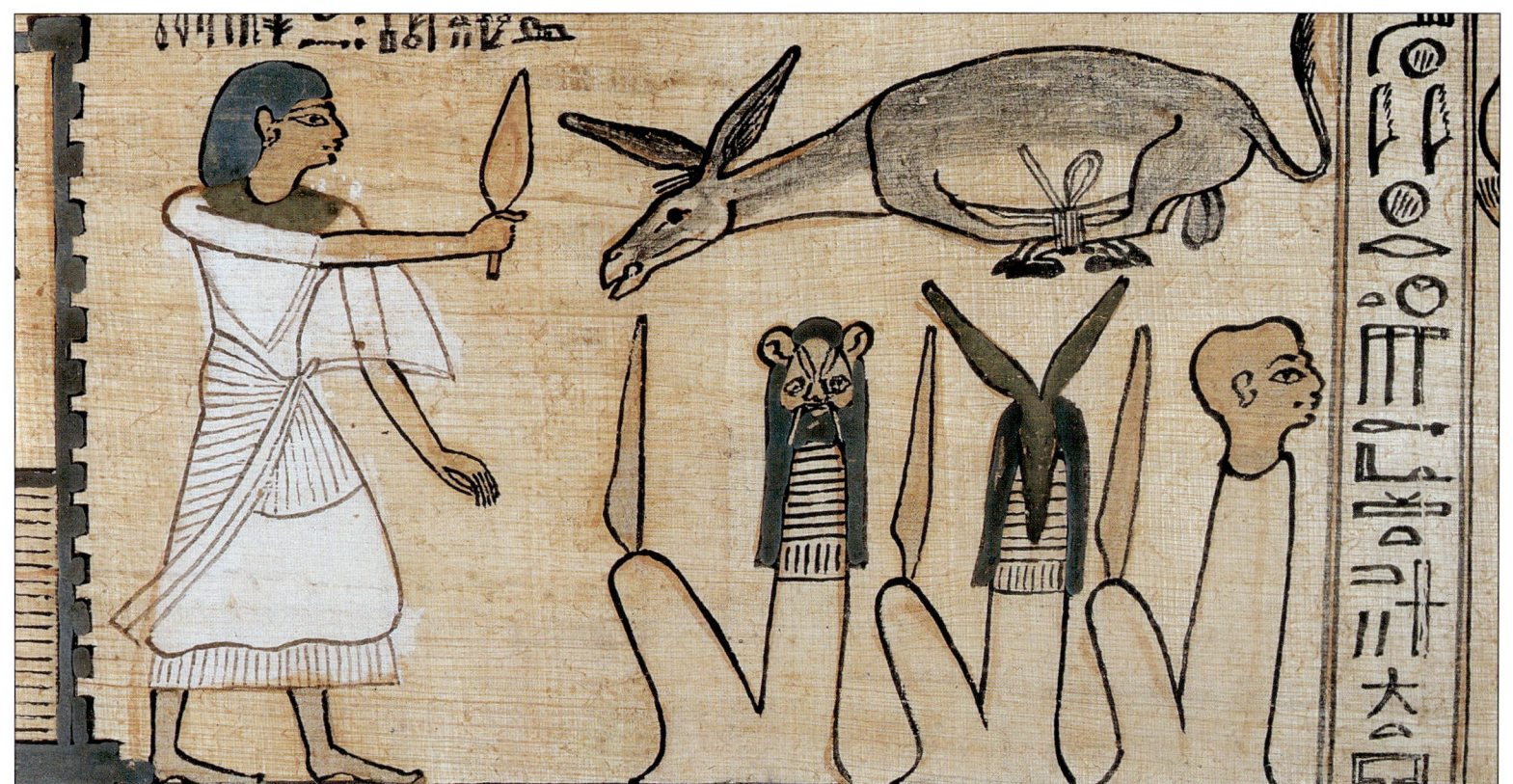

Household Deities

The two deities most closely associated with protection of the household and family life, especially women and children, were Bes and Taweret. They must have been close to the hearts of the ancient Egyptians, as they feature heavily in the various spells associated with illness and the hazards of everyday life. Like Heka (see *Magic*), no cult temple was dedicated to either of these deities, but their presence was ubiquitous in family life. Although they were associated with the relatively peaceful environment of the household, they could certainly be forces to be reckoned with. It was important to stay on the right side of these deities, by invoking them and making offerings to them. Both deities could be depicted looking surprisingly fierce, with teeth bared and tongue sticking out. It is thought that this may well have been for apotropaic reasons – that their aggressive expressions would scare away evil influences – and so their presence at particularly vulnerable times, such as childbirth and childhood, would have been deemed valuable. Bes was also thought to be able to ward off snakes from the house.

Bes the spirit-deity

It would probably be more correct to refer to Bes as a spirit or a benevolent demon than as a fully fledged deity. In fact, Bes may well have been a generic term for a number of protective demons. He was represented as a rather strange bandy-legged dwarf, with a lion's ears and mane, and a tail. He often wore a feathered headdress and an animal pelt over his back, and held a *sa* amulet of protection. His appearance ranged from jovial to really quite ferocious. He was often depicted playing musical instruments and hopping about, especially in the context of childbirth. His head appears in a protective capacity above the naked figure of the child Horus on the stelae known as *cippi* of Horus (see *Paraphernalia of Ritual*).

◀ *Taweret's name means 'the Great One'. In the magical texts she is sometimes referred to as 'sow' (*reret*).*

▲ *The female musician playing the lute on this faience dish has the image of the protective spirit Bes tattooed on her thigh. 18th Dynasty.*

The hippopotamus goddess

Taweret was portrayed as a hippopotamus standing on her hind legs, with a large stomach and pendulous breasts, so there was a clear visual association with pregnant women, and she could be called on to help every woman, whether royal or commoner, in childbirth. To heighten her apotropaic, or protective, capacity she was made to look more terrifying by having a crocodile tail on her back and a leonine muzzle, arms and legs. The most terrifying guise the ancient Egyptians could give a deity was as a composite animal incorporating elements of dangerous creatures, the prime example of which was the funerary demon Ammit (see *The Weighing of the Heart*). Taweret was often portrayed wearing a headdress composed of a low *modius* (a cylindrical headdress) surmounted by two plumes, sometimes with horns and a disc. She usually clutched a *sa, ankh* or *tyet*-amulet (see *Amulets*).

5953

◄ *Cosmetic spoons and dishes were often decorated with the image of a duck, which appears to have had erotic connotations. Bes was also a common motif on toilet objects and other personal possessions.*

particularly vulnerable time, not only to actual threats such as scorpions but also to ghosts and nightmares. In keeping with their apotropaic presence, Bes and Taweret were often depicted brandishing knives. The figure of Bes was also used as a tattoo, usually on the upper thigh of female singers and musicians. ◆

The persistence of tradition

The archaeological record at the site of Tell el-Amarna reveals that however radically the Eighteenth-Dynasty 'revolutionary' King Akhenaten (c.1352–c.1336 BC) attempted to change the state religion, there was no way that he was going to succeed in stamping out the traditional popular beliefs of the ancient Egyptian people. The presence of numerous amulets in the form of these domestic deities, and a stela depicting a mother and child worshipping Taweret (found under the stairs in one of the houses in the Main City) are good evidence for the continued reliance of the average person on the deities of most immediate importance in their lives. In the walled village at Tell el-Amarna, as well as in the tomb builders' village at Deir el-Medina, fragments of wall painting have been discovered in the main living rooms of some of the houses, which include Bes and Taweret in their design. Both deities were ever-present in the lives of most ordinary ancient Egyptian people.

Amulets and furniture

An incredible number of amulets in the miniature form of these deities have survived, so their popularity is evident. They were also incorporated into the design of furniture (especially beds), musical instruments, pottery and other vessels. Faience vessels have been found in the form of Taweret with a pouring hole in place of one of her nipples, and it is assumed that these would originally have contained milk. Images of Bes and Taweret on headrests would have been popular because sleep was considered a

Paraphernalia of Ritual

A variety of unusual objects have been discovered whose definite use and symbolic value will probably always remain uncertain. But this leaves us exciting scope for speculation. Rituals pertaining to the trials, tribulations and celebrations of everyday life would have been performed in the home, at shrines and at tombs or graves (especially those of relatives). The 'equipment' of popular ritual and belief included wands, amulets, votive objects, ceremonial vessels and a range of other artefacts, both inscribed and uninscribed.

Figurines

In the early twentieth century, the female figurines that today are called 'fertility figurines' were regarded as symbolic 'concubine figures' placed in tombs to service the sexual needs of the deceased male tomb owner. Closer scrutiny of the archaeological contexts of these objects has revealed that a larger number have actually been found in temple and domestic contexts than in tombs, so they were more frequently a ritual object of the living rather than of the dead.

Most are likely to have been votive offerings to deities such as the goddess of fertility, Hathor, and spirits of the dead particularly fathers, see *The Positive Influence of the Dead*. They may have been offerings from women who were unable to conceive, and who were seeking help from the divine or spirit world to solve their desperate problem. They tended to be made out of clay, wood or faience, and the emphasis in the fashioning of them was quite clearly on the pubic region and, to a lesser extent, the breasts. Sometimes the head was merely a 'pinch' of the clay, and the feet were rarely modelled. It has been suggested that this was a deliberate device to prevent the figurine from

▶ *The patterns on some female fertility figurines are thought to represent tattoos. Middle Kingdom.*

◀ *Over a dozen feminoform vessels have been found, all dating to the Eighteenth and Nineteenth Dynasties, and perhaps made to contain milk. They range from 11–17cm (4½–6½in) in height.*

▲ *By depicting the enemies of Egypt in a subdued state, it was believed this would magically become reality. Tutankhamun's ceremonial stool shows Syrians and Libyans on the top surface, and Nubians and Sudanese on its underside.*

leaving the place where it was deposited, since the ancient Egyptians believed in the magical creative properties of their religious imagery. We can be more certain of the purpose of these figurines when they were inscribed, usually with a woman's plea for a child (infertility was always regarded as a woman's problem).

There is evidence for private fertility cults that would have made use of a selection of ritual paraphernalia. A cache of votive material was discovered under the stairs of a house at the site of Tell el-Amarna, the ancient capital city of Akhetaten. The stash included a stela showing a woman and child worshipping the household goddess Taweret, two broken female figurines, and two model beds. It is impossible to tell whether these objects had been hidden here, were placed here for safekeeping, or whether this was in fact the location of a household shrine.

Another magical type of figurine was the execration figurine – a rough clay figure of a bound captive, often inscribed with a curse against a named foreign ruler, a group of people, or a particular place. The knowledge of a name was of magical significance and allowed the exercise of magical control over the possible threat of the foreigner. Often such a figure would be smashed in an execration ritual to destroy the power of the foreign ruler. Such execration texts were also sometimes inscribed on pottery bowls, which might be similarly ritually smashed and buried.

Ritual vessels

Various types of vessel clearly had a ritual significance, for example those in the form of pregnant and breast feeding women, and the deities Bes and Taweret. Pots have been discovered in the form of pregnant women with their hands rubbing their distended stomachs. These pots often date to the Eighteenth Dynasty (c.1550–c.1295 BC) and tend to be made of calcite (although there is a particularly

fine pottery example from Abydos in the Cairo Museum). The oil they contained would have been used to ease stretch marks and may have had some aromatherapeutic value, but the pots themselves would have also had a sympathetic magical significance. Several pots have been discovered with tampons painted on them. These were used to prevent miscarriage, and so a woman who possessed a feminoform vessel protected in this way would have hoped that she would benefit from the magical security it offered.

Pots dating to the Eighteenth and Nineteenth Dynasties (c.1550–c.1186 BC) have also been found in the form of breast-feeding women, sometimes with a spout in place of a nipple. Breast milk may have been stored in these vessels. Lactating women's milk was an important ingredient in several spells and remedies, indicating belief in its magical potency. It is possible that whatever the type of milk stored in a feminoform jar, it was believed to magically 'become' women's milk, and so might be used for magical purposes.

Cippi of Horus

Spells were often recorded on ritual objects, such as a type of stela known as a *cippus* of Horus. Examples that have survived tend to be made of stone or wood, and range in date from 1400 BC to the second century AD. The focus of each *cippus* was an image of the god Horus as a child (depicted naked and wearing the characteristic hairstyle of childhood, the 'sidelock of youth') triumphing over a selection of dangerous animals such as crocodiles, snakes and

◀ *The protective influence of the spirit-deity Bes was harnessed on the stelae called* cippi *of Horus used in the later period of Egyptian history, and held here by a healing statue inscribed with magical texts. Ptolemaic Period.*

Ritual gestures

A number of symbolic gestures occur repeatedly in illustrations of ancient Egyptian rituals. A magical protective gesture is illustrated in many tomb reliefs of the period c2400–1800BC. This was the pointing of the index finger and thumb at calves being born, for example, or cattle being driven through crocodile-infested water.

A ritual gesture described in magical texts was the placing of a hand on a patient or woman suffering in childbirth (the terminology implies that this was to 'seal' the vulnerable person in order to prevent harmful forces intruding.

scorpions. A representation of the head of the protective spirit-deity Bes tends to figure over Horus. Much of the rest of each *cippus* is covered in spells relating to dangers such as snakes and scorpions. The idea seems to have been that water (perhaps ideally rainwater) was poured over the *cippus* so that it would become magically imbued with the potency of the spells. The water could then be drunk or applied externally as a cure, antidote or preventative against hazards such as scorpion bites. Like breast milk, rainwater was considered to be of particular magical and medicinal effectiveness. For some reason we shall probably never know, it was thought to be especially effective in the healing of leg ailments.

Identical in purpose to the *cippi* were 'healing statues', of which a particularly fine example is that of Djedhor now in the Cairo Museum. He holds a *cippus*, but all the surfaces of Djedhor, himself, together with the plinth on which he kneels, are also covered in spells. Water was obviously meant to run over the statue because it sits in a collecting trough, and there is at least one channel for draining off the water. ◆

Wands

The most treasured possession of a practitioner of magic, such as a *Hery Seshta* ('Chief of Mysteries or Secrets'), would probably have been his wand. Three types have survived from ancient Egypt: the snake-shaped wand, the apotropaic (or protective wand) and the magic rod.

Snake-shaped wands were usually made of bronze. They could either be elongated, such as the Eighteenth-Dynasty example in the British Museum, London, or more coiled, such as the one dating to the First Intermediate Period (c.2181–c.2055 BC) in the Fitzwilliam Museum in Cambridge. It is possible that these wands were believed to represent the cobra-form goddess Weret Hekau ('Great of Magic'). Depictions of the divine personification of magic, Heka, show him holding two crossed snakes, and wooden and ivory figures masked like Bes or Beset, and connected with magic, hold metal snake wands. The Old Testament Book of Exodus records that the magicians attending Pharaoh performed the miracle of turning their wands into serpents.

Apotropaic wands
About 150 curved apotropaic wands have been found, mainly dating to the First Intermediate Period and Middle Kingdom (c.2181– c.1650

BC). They could be made of calcite, faience or ebony, but were usually of hippopotamus ivory. It is therefore possible that a deliberate association was being made with Taweret, the hippopotamus goddess. All manner of weird and wonderful magical imagery decorate these wands, including dancing baboons, snake-breathing lions, winged quadrupeds, human-headed winged snakes and sun discs on legs. More conventional representations of vultures, hippopotami, frogs and crocodiles also appear, as do depictions of protective *sa* and *udjat*-eye amulets and Seth, the god of chaos and infertility, as well as the apotropaic household deities Bes and Taweret, who are often shown wielding knives in a rather threatening fashion. Sometimes the terminal of the wand is adorned with the head of a leopard. When the wands are inscribed, the brief inscriptions are concerned with protection.

The inscriptions and imagery imply that these wands were used to benefit women and children, particularly at times of birth and early childhood. Their exact ritual purpose is uncertain. Perhaps they were placed or touched upon the pregnant woman or newborn child, or used to mark out a magic space in which the pregnant woman or mother and child would be protected from misfortune.

Magic rods
Similar imagery can be found on the magic rods that have survived from the Middle Kingdom and Second Intermediate periods of ancient

▶ *It is possible that the break in this ivory apotropaic wand was done deliberately before it was placed in a tomb. On its other side this wand is inscribed with a promise of protection for the Lady of the House, Seneb.*

Egyptian history (c.2055–c.1550 BC). Glazed steatite examples incorporate representations of frogs, turtles, baboons, crocodiles and felines, as well as lamps and amuletic symbols such as *sas* and *udjat*-eyes. These rods would have had miniature models of the animals attached to them using tiny pegs. We are not certain how they were employed, but they were presumably used to dominate the animals depicted on them, and turn their power into a protective rather than a malignant force. Some magical spells refer to the brandishing of a stick or a branch (the poor man's bronze or ivory wand), particularly in the commanding of malevolent spirits and demons. ◆

◀ *This coiled serpent wand was found in a tomb under the Ramesseum in western Thebes, tangled in a mass of hair.*

Amulets

Amulets were miniature devices believed to endow the owner or wearer with powers or magical protection. The ancient Egyptian words for 'amulet' – *sa*, *meket* and *nehet* – all derived from verbs meaning 'to guard' or 'to protect', while a fourth term – *wedja* – had the same sound as the word meaning 'well being'.

The earliest recognizable amulets date back to the Badarian phase of the Predynastic Period (c.5500–c.4000 BC). They have been found in graves, but it is likely that they were also considered useful to the owners during their lifetimes. We have no texts for the Predynastic Period, so cannot know the significance of these amulets. An amulet of an antelope's or gazelle's head, for example, might have been considered to be able to turn the owner into a successful hunter of the animal; it might have blessed the owner with the swiftness attributed to the animal; or if the animal was associated with evil, as it was later in Pharaonic history, it might have served an apotropaic purpose.

Stringing and knotting

Most amulets had a loop attached so that they could be suspended. Some rare examples of the original stringing have survived – intricately twisted and knotted thread made from flax fibres. The ancient Egyptians may have worn their amulets beautifully strung around their necks for all to see, but the evidence appears to indicate that they were probably knotted and bundled together and secreted somewhere safe on the person. We know that the tying and untying of knots were certainly very important in ancient Egyptian magic. The magico-medical texts record that

▶ *The decoration on Tutankhamun's chest includes the alternation of the* ankh *and the* was-*sceptre (symbolizing power) above the hieroglyphic sign of a basket meaning 'all'.*

amuletic images were sometimes painted or drawn on linen placed on the patient's body. Or they could be drawn directly on the patient's hand and then licked off. We also learn from the texts that certain spells were to be recited over very specific amulets. Spell 30 of the magical text on Papyrus Leiden 1,348, had to be recited four times over a 'dwarf of clay' placed on the forehead of a woman suffering from a difficult labour. This would probably have been an amulet of the dwarf spirit-deity Bes.

Miniature representations of deities such as Bes, Taweret and Hathor were acquired to ensure the protection and influences of the divine world. Other popular amulets were the scarab, with its creative and solar associations, the protective *udjat* or Eye of Horus, associated with wholeness and healing, and the *tyet* (see *Funerary Amulets*).

The *tyet*-amulet was particularly important for the protection of women during pregnancy and childbirth, because it was associated with Isis and,

▲ *The best known of all ancient Egyptian amulets is the scarab, examples of which have been found made of every material known to the Egyptians.*

more specifically, with her blood. We cannot be certain of its meaning but it is knot shaped. It possibly represented the knotted girdle of the goddess, or it has also been suggested that it represented a tampon inserted into Isis when she was pregnant so that she would not miscarry

▲ *The* ankh, djed, *and* was *amuletic signs are often found together, with the symbolic meaning of 'life, stability and power'. This collar belonged to Khnumit, daughter of the 12th-Dynasty king Amenemhat II.*

or so that her wicked brother Seth could not harm the son she was carrying. It would therefore have been hoped that by sympathetic magic, the owner or wearer of the amulet would also be protected against miscarriage.

Two other amulets that would have been particularly meaningful in popular religion were the *ankh* and the *sa*. The *ankh* was the hieroglyphic symbol for 'life' (or perhaps, more specifically, the life-giving elements of air and water), and may have represented a sandal strap, or perhaps a more elaborate knot or bow. The *sa* was an amulet of protection, and may have represented a mobile papyrus shelter, tied up for transportation – vital protection against the sun for anyone who worked out in the fields or desert. The household deities Bes and Taweret were often depicted standing, resting their front paws on *sa* amulets.

As might be expected, these amulets were included in the decoration of magical implements such as apotropaic wands and magic rods (see *Wands*), and ceremonial devices such as the sistrum (see *Music and Dance in Religion*).

They were also included in the design of more secular objects, such as furniture, musical instruments, vessels, cosmetic spoons and mirrors. Other amulets included cowrie shells (either the actual shells or imitations of them made from other materials), which were often strung to make girdles, worn by women to protect their fertility; parts of animals such as claws and hairs from a cat; and models of parts of the human body, plants or animals.

Oracular amuletic decrees

During the late New Kingdom and Third Intermediate Period (c.1100–c.747 BC), amulets also took the form of short spells written on tiny pieces of papyrus rolled up inside cylindrical tubes, designed so that they could be worn around the neck. The text usually read as if it were a proclamation by a deity or the gods in general, promising to protect the wearer and threatening divine retribution to those who endangered him or

▶ *The frog was a symbol of creation, fertility, birth and regeneration. This amulet dates to the 1st Dynasty, but much later on, the Christianized Egyptians adopted the frog as a symbol of the resurrection.*

her. One Twenty-second Dynasty example of an oracular amuletic decree in the British Museum, London, declares:

We shall fill her womb with male and female children. We shall save her...from miscarrying, and from giving birth to twins.

Often it is obvious that the wearers were children, whose fates were decreed by the gods at birth. They were promised long life, good health, lots of possessions, and protection against demons, foreign sorcerers, the Evil Eye and harmful manifestations of the deities. ◆

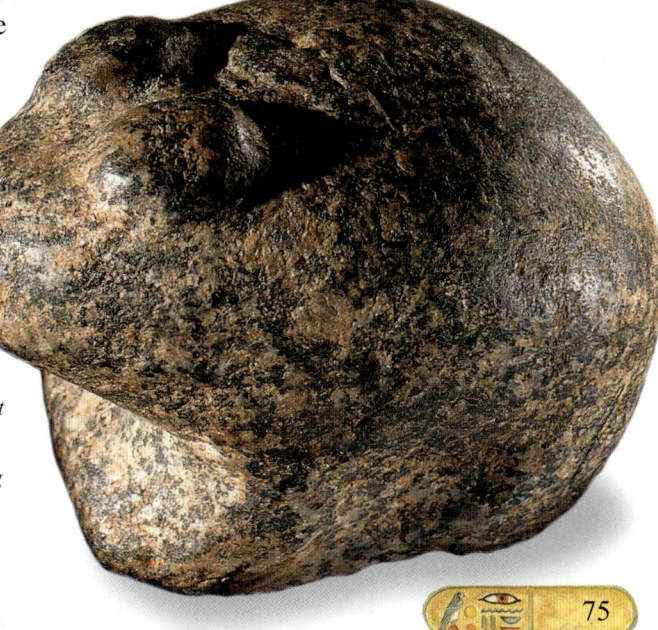

Rites of Passage

Women in society

The primary role of ancient Egyptian women was to have children and to run the household. Ordinary women did their share of hard physical work, such as gathering in the harvest and grinding the corn. They tended to be responsible for food production and were employed as musicians, dancers, acrobats and mourners, among other jobs. Women did not hold public office and it is unlikely than many of them were literate. A woman's status largely depended on that of her husband, but we do know that women of the higher social class were able to sit on local tribunals; witness documents, execute their own last testament; inherit, buy, administer and sell property; free slaves; adopt children; and sue.

In all cultures, the transitional stages of the human life cycle are vulnerable times, coinciding with the fundamental changes from non-pregnant to pregnant, from foetus to child, and from child to adult. The ancient Egyptians believed that rituals were necessary to help them through the precarious phases of pregnancy, childbirth, early childhood and puberty. All of these, if attained without mishap, were marked by celebrations that involved giving thanks to the gods.

Fertility rituals

A woman's ability to conceive was of paramount importance to the security of her marriage, her social standing, and the comfort of her spirit after death. She would not have fulfilled her expected role in society if she died before bearing children. For this reason it is hardly surprising that childless women should turn to the divine or spirit world for a solution to their problem. There is much evidence of fertility rituals, both within the house – involving imagery of Bes and Taweret (see *Household Deities*) – and at sacred places such as tombs, temples and shrines, involving votive offerings such as fertility figurines (see *Paraphernalia of Ritual*).

Both household deities and great state gods and goddesses, such as the cow goddess Hathor and the ithyphallic god Min, were closely associated with fertility (both of the Egyptian people and of the land). During the Graeco-Roman period, if not earlier, women seem to have exposed their genitals before the cult statue of Hathor in an attempt to assimilate the goddess's fertility. Various amulets were worn, or made as votive offerings, to ensure fertility. These included tiny representations of the deities Bes, Taweret and Hathor, as well as model penises, breasts and female genitals.

An absence of menstruation was clearly linked to pregnancy. Both menstrual and birth blood must have been considered to be impure because women were expected to perform purification rituals after both of these events. Pregnant women were thought to be particularly susceptible to the ill effects caused by harmful spirits and demons. Spells were devised to prevent the demon personification of death from having sexual intercourse with a pregnant woman – a violation that would have had adverse effects on the unborn child.

Ensuring a trouble-free birth

Rituals were performed to ensure that the expectant mother had a trouble-free pregnancy and

▼ *In addition to free-standing fertility figurines, examples exist of limestone or terracotta figures of naked women lying on model beds (sometimes decorated with convolvulus), often with a child (usually male) beside her thigh or being suckled.*

birth, to speed up the labour, to safeguard the newborn baby, and to guarantee the mother an adequate supply of milk. These often involved reciting a particular spell at the appropriate time. Associated with the significance of knots in ancient Egyptian magic, the woman probably bound up her hair very tightly when the baby was due, so that it could be loosened during labour, thereby sympathetically releasing the baby from the womb. Certain props were also used in the popular ritual at birth, such as amulets and apotropaic wands.

Women had their babies squatting on bricks or sitting on a wooden birthing stool. Like all that was of greatest importance in the lives of the ancient Egyptians, the birth brick was divinely personified as the goddess Meskhent. She was depicted as a brick with a human head, or as a woman wearing a headdress consisting of a brick or a peculiar emblem. This may have represented the forked uterus of a cow (or perhaps two long palm shoots with curved tips), or a *peshesh-kaf* knife (a flint fishtailed knife that was used to cut the umbilical cord). It was thought that the goddess predetermined the lives of newborn babies, and their fates were ritually inscribed or recited over the bricks.

Sympathetic magic was also used during childbirth. Spell 28 of the magical text written on Papyrus Leiden 1,348 declares: 'Hathor, the Lady of Dendera is the one giving birth.' This meant that Hathor would give birth, and in so doing suffer on behalf of the woman who was actually in labour; a transfer of pain was believed to take place. The playing of musical instruments, singing and dancing also appear to have been important at the time of childbirth.

It may be that the fragments of wall painting found in houses at Deir el-Medina and the workmen's village at

Tell el-Amarna portray the period of confinement and celebration following a successful birth. The scenes include parts of figures of the household spirit-deity Bes; a dancing female flute player with a Bes tattoo on her thigh and the convolvulus plant (which was associated with fertility) around her; a child; the lower part of a naked kneeling woman with convolvulus and a servant girl. The

▲ *Hathor, Lady of Dendera, retains a reputation for helping women who have fertility problems to this very day. Egyptian women who want children still visit the crypts of her temple.*

paintings decorated mudbrick platforms, today referred to as 'box-beds'. It has been suggested that these beds were where women gave birth or nursed their newborn babies, but they may well have

▲ *Rectangular mudbrick 'box-bed' structures (which would originally have been plastered and painted or whitewashed) have been found in the corner of the front room of 28 of the 68 houses excavated at Deir el-Medina.*

▼ *The mother and child on this ostracon have been drawn in a 'confinement pavilion' surrounded by convolvulus.*

been ordinary beds, or altars (or neither). The subjects of the paintings are similar to those found on *ostraca* (inscribed pieces of pottery or limestone flakes) from Deir el-Medina.

We know from one of the *Tales of Wonder*, a collection of stories composed during the Middle Kingdom (c.2055–c.1650 BC) and found on Papyrus Westcar, that beer-drinking was considered to be obligatory after childbirth. But first the mother and child had to undergo a period of confinement or separation from the outside world. The end of this period of 14 days was marked by ritual cleansing and by eating a honey cake that was thought to keep demons at bay and to stabilize and strengthen the mother.

Breast feeding provided essential nourishment for the newborn baby. A lactating woman could ensure or stimulate her milk supply by wearing an amulet in the form of the rising moon. Amulets in the shape of breasts have also been found. Lactating women were credited with *heka* (see *Magic*), and breast milk (especially that of a woman who had given birth to a male child) was considered to be a potent ingredient in a number of the magico-medical texts (especially in remedies for colds, eye problems and burns).

Vulnerability in early childhood

In addition to the predictions made about a baby at his or her birth, it was believed that a baby's viability was indicated by its first utterance. If it was '*ny*' it would live, and if it was '*embi*' it was bound to die. Infant mortality was indeed high in ancient Egypt, and early childhood was a vulnerable time. The texts known as the *Incantations for Mother and Child*, found on Papyrus Berlin 3027, consist of two books of spells and prescriptions for the treatment of infant illnesses, and for the protection of children against demons and the dead. It was feared that female spirits might try to snatch the infant from his or her mother (see *The Negative Influence of the Dead*). One of the spells is intended to cure a child of a fever. It is entitled 'Spell for a Knot' and was to be recited:

...over the pellet of gold, the forty bread pellets, and the cornelian sealstone, with the crocodile and the hand. To be strung on a strip of fine linen; made into an amulet; placed on the neck of the child.

A child's name was vital to his or her personal identity. The names given at birth could reflect several popular religious practices, including the

celebration of festivals of particular deities, such as *Hathoremheb* ('Hathor is in festival'), and the consultation of oracles during pregnancy, for example *DjedDjehutyiwefankh* ('Thoth says he will live'). Others were devised to protect the child from harm, for instance *Amunhedebirtbint*, which means 'Amun kills the evil eye'.

Rituals of puberty
The ability to produce offspring was presumably the deciding factor in the transition from childhood to adulthood. Rituals probably accompanied a girl's first menstruation, but very little is known about ancient Egyptian puberty rituals. Any symbolic or ritual recognition of attaining adulthood quite possibly involved the cutting off of the 'sidelock' – the hairstyle often worn by young children. There is also some evidence for the circumcision of pubescent boys. The Sixth-Dynasty tomb of Ankhmahor, the 'royal architect', at Saqqara contains what appears to be a scene of a young boy (aged about ten or twelve) being circumcised. The inscription on a stela from Naga ed-Deir, now in the Oriental Institute in Chicago, claims that the owner was circumcised together with 120 others. Another First Intermediate Period inscription (c.2181–c.2055 BC), this time in the tomb of Mereri in Dendera, tells us that Mereri was proud of having circumcised the youths of the town. Certainly by the Twenty-fifth Dynasty (c.747 BC), circumcision was associated with purity.

Marriage would have formalized adulthood because it meant that women could begin to produce children. Consequently marriage, at least for a woman, probably took place in her early teens, so that she could conceive as soon after her first menstruation as possible.

▲ *The man performing this ritual circumcision operation is identified as a* ka-*priest, but this may well have been an honorary title for élite men of various occupations or official positions.*

As far as we know there was no religious marriage ceremony, but a celebration would have accompanied the initiation of a new household, and the first step towards the formation of a new family unit (the basis of the ancient Egyptian social structure). Marriage – at least for those with property and disposable wealth – was marked by the drawing up of a contract, which supplied the woman with a number of rights and benefits. The surviving agreements show that divorce was socially acceptable, that women remained in possession of their dowries, and that divorced women could expect compensation from their ex-husbands. ◆

Maat

Maat was the principle that held ancient Egyptian society together and underpinned religious belief. The word is usually translated as 'truth', 'order', 'justice' or 'balance'. To recognize abstract concepts in their system of beliefs, the ancient Egyptians felt a need to divinely personify them and this they did with *maat*, which was represented as the goddess Maat, a woman with an ostrich feather on her head.

The idea of *maat* as universal order or harmony corresponds with the most

▲ *In a funerary context the goddess Maat was often depicted with large enveloping wings – much associated with protective female deities – as here in the tomb of the 19th-Dynasty king Sethnakhte in west Thebes.*

fundamental role of the reigning king. This was to maintain *maat* on a national level by building temples and making offering to the gods (in fact, the ancient Egyptian deities were said to live off *maat*) and thereby placating them; by exercising control over the potential enemies of Egypt (which basically amounted to all foreigners); and by controlling nature (especially wild animals). Life in Egypt was thought to be

characterized by *maat*, whereas outside its borders *isfet* reigned, that is chaos, epitomized by the desert, wild animals, foreign lands and foreign people.

The moral code

The ideal was to lead a life in accordance with *maat*, corresponding to the socially acceptable or ethical way to behave. The texts of the Wisdom Literature reveal that certain crimes were considered crimes against *maat*. These included disorder, rebellion, envy, deceit, greed, laziness, injustice and ingratitude. The Old Kingdom *Writings of Ptahhotep* declare that 'Maat is great and lasting in effect'.

Wisdom literature

There is a body of surviving literature from ancient Egypt, known today as Instructive or Wisdom Literature. It tended to be written as if by a father for his son, or by a tutor for his pupil, and it tells us how a young boy was expected to lead his life correctly – a code of moral values that would have acted as a check on human behaviour.

The text known as the *Writings of Ptahhotep* was attributed to a vizier of the Fifth Dynasty, but its earliest appearance is in a papyrus dating from the Twelfth Dynasty. It offers a series of maxims to be followed to achieve success in life, based on the ideal of an existence in accordance with the principle of *maat*.

The *Instruction of King Amenemhat I* was written as if the dead king is speaking in a revelation to his son and successor Senusret I. It warns Senusret of disloyalty among the courtiers, and emphasizes the contrast between the divinity of kingship and the limitations of a mortal king, between the ideal – embodied in the concept of *maat* – and the realities of life.

▲ *In the Middle Kingdom Maat, was described as being at the nostrils of Re, while by the 18th Dynasty she was being called 'daughter of Re'. This tomb scene at Deir el-Medina dates to the 19th Dynasty.*

The emphasis was very much on how people should listen as opposed to being deaf to *maat*, and on the idea that greed destroys social relations. In the Middle Kingdom *Tale of the Eloquent Peasant*, the lazy and the greedy are said to be deaf to *maat*.

If, when he died, a man wanted it known that he had spoken truthfully and had acted in accordance with justice, thus maintaining social harmony, he would have a recurring formula inscribed on his tomb: 'I have spoken *maat*, I have accomplished *maat*.'

The concept of *maat* and the importance of living a just life was central to the beliefs about judgment after death – when the dead person's heart was weighed in the balance against *maat*, symbolized by the feather worn on the head of the goddess Maat.

Justice for all?

The concept of justice for all is apparent in the textual evidence from ancient Egypt and in theory everyone in Egypt had access to a fair hearing. The author of the *Instruction for Merikare*, written during the Middle Kingdom (c.2055–c.1650 BC) advised the new king to 'make no difference between a man of position and a commoner'. Later on, in the New Kingdom (c.1550–c.1069 BC), the viziers were being instructed, 'See equally the man you know and the man you don't know, the man who is near you and the man who is far away.' As overseer of the courts of Egypt, the vizier held the title, 'Priest of Maat'.

Of course, in practice it would be very surprising to find a society in which position, influence and wealth did not count for anything. Bribery was probably common practice, because in another piece of instructive literature dating to the Ramesside period, the author Amenemope felt it necessary to write: 'Do not accept the reward of the powerful man, and persecute the weak for him.'

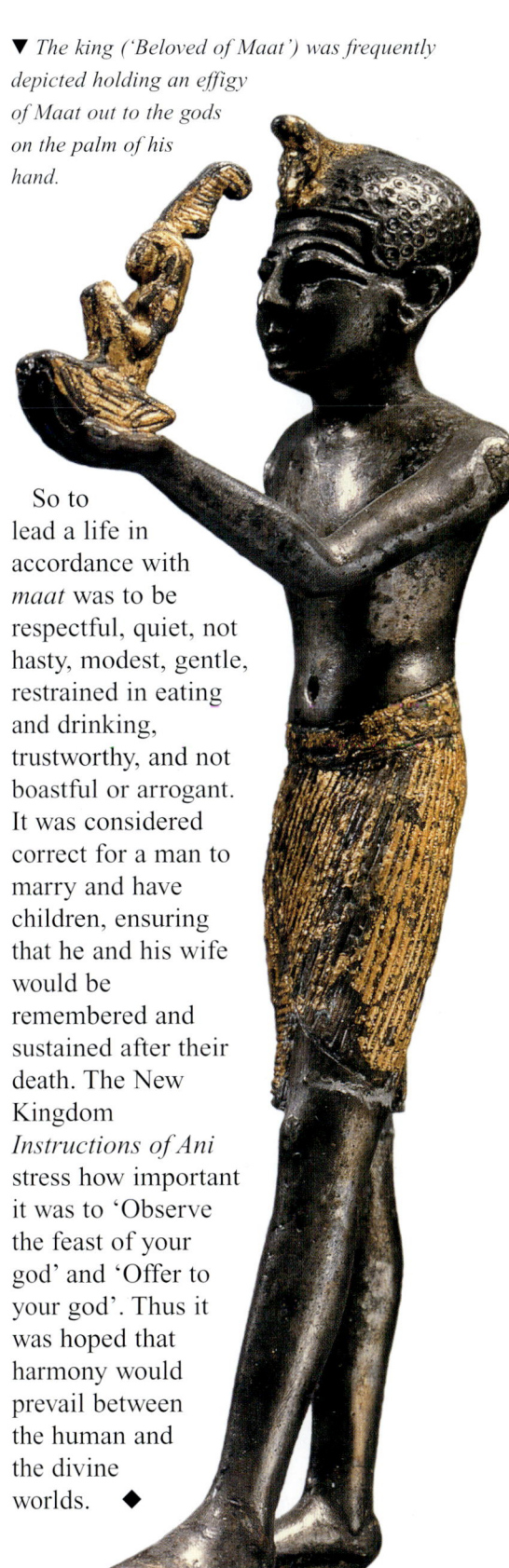

▼ *The king ('Beloved of Maat') was frequently depicted holding an effigy of Maat out to the gods on the palm of his hand.*

So to lead a life in accordance with *maat* was to be respectful, quiet, not hasty, modest, gentle, restrained in eating and drinking, trustworthy, and not boastful or arrogant. It was considered correct for a man to marry and have children, ensuring that he and his wife would be remembered and sustained after their death. The New Kingdom *Instructions of Ani* stress how important it was to 'Observe the feast of your god' and 'Offer to your god'. Thus it was hoped that harmony would prevail between the human and the divine worlds. ◆

Dreams

The ancient Egyptians believed that what they dreamed had a bearing on their daily lives, and that the interpretation of dreams was a valid means of predicting the future. A collection of texts has survived from ancient Egypt, which are known today as 'Dream Books'. They consist of lists of possible dream scenarios and what the dreams indicate will happen in the life of the dreamer. For example, if

▶ *Hatshepsut's mortuary temple at Deir el-Bahri is set in a deep bay in the desert cliffs which were in turn at the foot of the pyramidal peak sacred to the goddesses Hathor and Mertseger.*

A dream directory

The Dream Book of qenherkhepshef discovered at Deir el-Medina is written in tabular form, with the dreams described in one column of text and interpretation in another:

If a man sees himself in a dream...

...submerging in the river: good: this means purification from all evils.

...eating crocodile: good: this means acting as an official among his people.

...burying an old man: good: this means flourishing.

...seeing his face in a mirror: bad: this means another wife.

...shod with white sandals: bad: this means roaming the earth.

...copulating with a woman: bad: this means mourning.

...his bed catching fire: bad: this means driving away his wife.

someone dreamt that he was drinking warm beer, it was thought to forewarn that the dreamer would soon suffer harm. A careful reading of the texts in the original shows that many of the correlations between the content of the dream and the prophecy are based on the use of puns (a potent form of magic). For instance, to dream about a harp meant that something evil would surely happen to the person in question; whereas to dream about a donkey indicated that the dreamer was soon to be promoted. To get a sense of the magical use of language in these predictions we have to know that the ancient Egyptian word for 'harp' was *benet*, and the word for 'evil' was *bint*; that the word for 'donkey' was *aa* and the word for 'to be promoted' was *saa*.

Who would actually have been in possession of these books? Did certain priests and magicians own them? Or might a family have had its own copy of such a manual in their home, ready to consult whenever they felt the need? We know that the scribe Qenherkhepshef, who was in charge of the administration of Deir el-Medina in the late thirteenth and early twelfth centuries BC, owned one. Today it is known as Papyrus Chester Beatty III. It is written in

▶ *From at least the beginning of the Old Kingdom, the ancient Egyptians used headrests to support their heads while they slept. The presence of the protective spirit-deity Bes in the design of Tutankhamun's headrest is apotropaic.*

▲ *As 'Lady of the West', Hathor was protectress of the west Theban necropolis. She was depicted on stelae and funerary papyri as a cow leaving the desert to come down into the papyrus marshes and she acted as a link between the tombs and life in the Nile Valley.*

the hieratic script and is now in the British Museum in London. Although it dates to the Ramesside Period, it has been noticed that the language used is very Middle Kingdom in style, and so perhaps it is a copy of a text originally compiled in the Eleventh or Twelfth Dynasty. The library of this particular scribe was pretty impressive, including as it did, examples of poetry, literature, history, magical spells and a Calendar of Lucky and Unlucky Days.

The Lector Priests would have acted as the link between the temples and the local communities. Their role in the temple was associated with the written and spoken word in the form of spells and incantations, and they were closely associated with magic throughout Egyptian history. Apart from their ritual duties, they had a reputation as interpreters of dreams. They presumably consulted these 'Dream Books'.

▶ *Tuthmosis IV recorded his dream in which the Great Sphinx appeared to him in all its aspects – Khepri-Re-Atum – on the stela he set up between the paws of the Sphinx.*

◀ *Imhotep, the architect of the Step Pyramid at Saqqara, was deified during the Late Period and was one of the patron deities of the healing sanctuary in Hatshepsut's mortuary temple.*

Fear of nightmares

Because dreams were believed to be of such great significance, it becomes clear why the Egyptians were so concerned about nightmares and attempted to guard against them with spells and apotropaic headrests. Papyrus Chester Beatty III suggests using protective spells on waking from a nightmare, and examples of headrests have been found decorated with images of the protective household deities Bes and Taweret (sometimes brandishing knives against any possible threat to the sleeper).

The magical papyri of the Ptolemaic Period explained to people how they could go about directing the anger of the god Seth against their enemies, causing them nightmares or even death. It was thought possible to cause someone much upset and trauma by sending them dreams of ill omen.

Incubation

During the first millennium BC, a practice known as 'incubation' became popular. People went to sleep in structures known as sanatoria or healing sanctuaries, built specifically for this purpose inside the precincts of temples, in order to have healing or helpful

dreams, particularly to help to solve infertility problems. Part of the Eighteenth-Dynasty ruler Hatshepsut's mortuary temple at Deir el-Bahri was converted into one such sanatorium. It was dedicated to the two deified sages Imhotep (the vizier and chief royal architect during the reign of the Third-Dynasty king Djoser (c.2667–c.2648 BC)) and Amenhotep, son of Hapu, a high official during the reign of the Eighteenth-Dynasty king Amenhotep III (c.1390–c.1352 BC).

In the story of Setne Khaemwese and Si-Osire, written in demotic on papyrus and dating to the Roman Period, Mehusekhe, the wife of Setne, seeks a solution to her inability to conceive. She spends a night in a sanctuary where she has a dream in which she is advised to concoct and take a remedy made from the crushed gourds of a melon vine. This she does, but it is also clearly stated that she must have sexual intercourse with her husband and, as a result, she becomes pregnant.

There were some occasions on which gods were said to have appeared to people in dreams and in this way to have affected or sanctioned a particular decision (a form of oracular consultation). During the New Kingdom (c.1550–c.1069 BC), one Theban official was said to have been inspired by the goddess Hathor in a dream to build his tomb in a certain place. ◆

Oracles

The earliest unambiguous evidence that the ancient Egyptians consulted oracles dates from the New Kingdom (c.1550–c.1069 BC). It takes the form of papyri, and – more often – ostraca, the pieces of pottery or limestone on which scribes took notes, from the tomb-builders' village of Deir el-Medina on the west bank of the River Nile at Thebes. At Deir el-Medina it was usually the oracle of the tomb-builders' royal patron deity Amenhotep I that was consulted. His shrine was located just outside the village, to the north.

Oracles tended to be consulted on certain festival days, when the cult statue of the god was carried in procession out of his or her shrine or temple on the shoulders of a number of priests. An expression that regularly occurs in the records as an introduction to a description of the consultation with the deity is the phrase 'As I stood before (him)'. However, although the ordinary person might have come closer to a cult statue during this festival procession than at any time (it was usually in the temple), it was still always concealed from view, often in a barque shrine.

Ostraca now in the British Museum, London, reveal that oracles were used mainly in disputes over property (especially houses and tombs). They might also be consulted to end a disagreement between a buyer and a seller. On Ostracon 576 from Deir el-Medina, it is recorded that the buyer asked the oracle to specify the amount of grain he ought to receive because a certain tradesman had the reputation of sneakily reducing it. Sometimes advice or questions were asked of the oracle. Ostracon 562 records the specific question: 'Should I go North?' In this way we are able to learn something of the mundane problems and indecisions of ordinary life, and the comfort to be gained from having the gods endorse everyday decision-making.

Oracular judgement

Oracles were also considered useful for helping to solve crimes, and for bringing the guilty to justice. In the case of a robbery, a list of suspects might be named before the god, and he then had to indicate the guilty suspect. Ostracon 4 from Deir el-Medina records that two articles of clothing had been stolen from a man. The houses of the possible thieves were named in front of the cult statue of Amenhotep I, and when that of the scribe Amen-nakht was named the god made a sign of affirmation. The scribe was summoned to a tribunal (*kenbet*) with his daughter, who was in fact found to be the thief. So the local oracle and the court would have strengthened each other's decision-making in the judicial process.

The ancient texts are ambiguous about the way the oracles gave their answers, but there were various ways in which a god might have made his decisions known: by the priests speaking; by mechanical manipulation inside the statue, such as the movement of the head; by the statue carried by the priests moving forwards or backwards; or by the god approaching an affirmative or negative piece of writing placed on

▲ *On festival days the barque shrine of Amun was processed on the shoulders of priests, as shown here in a relief from Hatshepsut's chapel at Karnak. It was on these occasions that the oracle of the god might be consulted.*

either side of the processional way. In the previously mentioned case of the names of the houses possibly sheltering the thief, the names may have been written on reed strips, with the god then somehow guiding the decision as to which one was drawn.

The word of the oracle does not seem to have necessarily been final (it was obviously not automatically accepted as law). Two separate papyri exist that each refer to the same dispute, with a lapse of three years between them, indicating that it was still being debated. If the response given by one oracle was not what the petitioner wanted to hear, it appears to have been possible for him to go on to consult other deities. Even so, it seems to have been usual for those consulting oracles to be called upon to swear oaths binding them to the oracle's decision: in view of this it may be that the ancient Egyptians were not quite so fearful of their gods as we often assume them to have been. ◆

Festivals and Pilgrimages

Festivals were occasions of celebration – of music, dancing, eating and drinking. They were also times when ordinary people might benefit from a closer encounter with the cult statue of a deity than was usually possible. For most of the time, the cult statue resided in a shrine in the dimly lit inner sanctuary of a temple – a place forbidden to the impure and uninitiated. But on festival days, the statue was carried in procession out of the temple, accompanied by musicians, singers, dancers, acrobats and incense burners. People might have come close to the statue, but still would not have seen it because it was carefully hidden from the masses. During a festival they might be given the opportunity to commune with the deity by consulting its oracle. This gave them a chance to consult the god for his wisdom on an issue that was important to their daily lives, such as whether it was a good time to make a long and difficult journey. The divine go-ahead was sought. A god might also be asked to settle a dispute or indicate the person responsible for a crime.

Calendars of festivals

The Hour Priests working in the House of Life in each of the temples worked out the annual calendar of festivals around which the temple's year revolved. Some of the calendars have survived; for example, in the Festival Hall of the Eighteenth-Dynasty king Tuthmosis III (c.1479–c.1425 BC) at Karnak temple, 54 feast days are

listed for one year. And at Ramesses III's mortuary temple at Medinet Habu, 60 festivals are listed. We learn from this 'calendar of feasts and offerings' that 84 loaves of bread were required for a monthly festival, and almost 4,000 for the national Festival of Sokar, the Memphite funerary deity.

The focus of some festivals was the visitation by one deity on another. The cow goddess Hathor, for example, left her main cult centre at Dendera each year to journey by boat to Edfu, where she was united with the

▲ *Many ostraca depicting figures like this female acrobat originate from the tomb-builders' village of Deir el-Medina.*

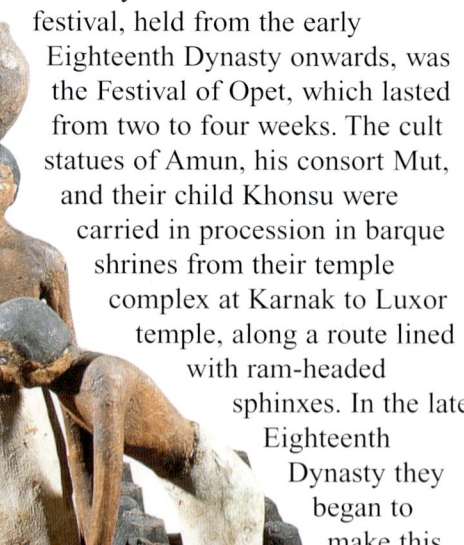

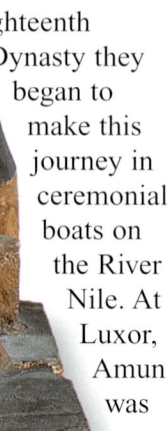

falcon deity Horus. Another annual festival, held from the early Eighteenth Dynasty onwards, was the Festival of Opet, which lasted from two to four weeks. The cult statues of Amun, his consort Mut, and their child Khonsu were carried in procession in barque shrines from their temple complex at Karnak to Luxor temple, along a route lined with ram-headed sphinxes. In the late Eighteenth Dynasty they began to make this journey in ceremonial boats on the River Nile. At Luxor, Amun was

▶ *Bread and beer were the staples of the Egyptian diet, and wooden models such as this one were intended to ensure their production for eternity. Middle Kingdom.*

▲ *In this tomb painting the cones balanced on the heavy black wigs of these women revellers at a banquet symbolize sweet-smelling ointments. They also wear jewellery and fine clothing.*

believed to have sexual intercourse with the mother of the reigning king so that she would give birth to the royal *ka*. The king was then united with his *ka* in the sanctuary of the temple, and he was believed to emerge as a god.

The dead were also involved in important festivals such as the Beautiful Festival of the Valley, which lasted 12 days and was celebrated from the early Eighteenth Dynasty onwards. The divine family of Karnak left their east-bank temple and crossed the river to visit Deir el-Bahri, and later, another mortuary temple as well. Ordinary people celebrated this festival at their family burial place by sharing a meal with the spirits of their dead relatives.

Revelry at Bubastis

People made pilgrimages to the more important festivals. Writing in the mid fifth century BC, Herodotus recorded the journeying of pilgrims to the cult site of Bubastis in the eastern Delta, to celebrate the festival of the cat goddess Bastet. He described the trip to Bubastis by boat, during which the women on the river hurled abuse at women on the banks, danced, hitched up their skirts, and exposed their genitals to the world

around them. This bawdy behaviour was probably meant to pass fertility from the women to the land (or vice versa). We know that on other occasions women exposed themselves before a statue of the goddess Hathor, hoping to benefit from the goddess's close association with fertility.

Herodotus wrote that 700,000 people (excluding children) attended the festival of Bastet. People sang and musical instruments such as the flute and castanets were played. Sacrifices were made, and more wine was drunk than during all the rest of the year.

Probably the cult centre most commonly visited by

▶ *A married couple are depicted on this limestone stela from Abydos. The man holds a* sekhem *sceptre in his right hand, denoting 'power' and 'might'.*

pilgrims was Abydos, the legendary burial place and chief temple of Osiris, the god of the dead, the Afterlife, rebirth and vegetation. During the Middle Kingdom (c.2055–c.1650 BC), thousands of people went to Abydos and set up private stelae in cenotaphs and tombs around the temple of Osiris, hoping to ensure a never-ending participation in the festivals of the god. These stelae also functioned as family monuments, and for this reason repeated pilgrimages were made, both to the temple of Osiris and to these memorials to the deceased. Scenes on the walls of New Kingdom private tombs often depict a symbolic pilgrimage being made by the dead person to Abydos. ◆

Music and Dance in Egyptian Religion

Singers, dancers and musicians were an important part of temple life. People believed that the gods enjoyed, and were pacified by, singing, music and dance. In the New Kingdom *Teachings of Ani*, song, dance and incense are described as the food of the gods. These activities accompanied the daily temple rites, figured highly at festivals and formed a part of more personal religious rituals – during funerals and at childbirth, for example. No musical notation has survived from ancient Egypt, but we do have the words of songs; illustrations of musicians, singers and dancers; the titles of people in these professions; and ancient musical instruments such as the harp, lute, lyre, flute, double reed-pipe, drum, cymbals, tambourine, bells and a form of guitar.

Temple musicians

If temple musicians played before the cult statues of the gods, we can assume that they would not have been allowed to lay their eyes upon the statues (because only the king and High Priest were in a position to do this). It has therefore been suggested that any musicians allowed into the inner sanctuary were quite likely to have been blind. Male harpists depicted on the walls of tombs do occasionally appear to be blind, and disability does not seem to have been considered a bar to purity; there is no reason to believe that people with physical disabilities were ostracized by ancient Egyptian society.

At festivals, musicians, singers and dancers walked in procession out of the temple with the shrine housing the cult statue. Often the point was not to produce pleasing music, but a rhythmic sound to create a state of religious ecstasy – or simply a loud noise to scare away harmful spirits, for example at birth. Clappers and *sistra* were the two instruments most useful for these purposes. Clappers were usually made of

ivory, which meant that they were curved like apotropaic wands. They often had a design carved into them, such as a shrine, a woman's head or the head of Hathor (some texts describe this goddess as 'Lady of Dance'). *Sistra* were ceremonial rattles, which were

▲ *The double reed-pipe was played by female musicians accompanying dancers at festive occasions. 18th Dynasty.*

▼ *Hathor was 'Lady of the Vulva' and the 'Hand of Atum': the combination in these clappers probably had sexual connotations.*

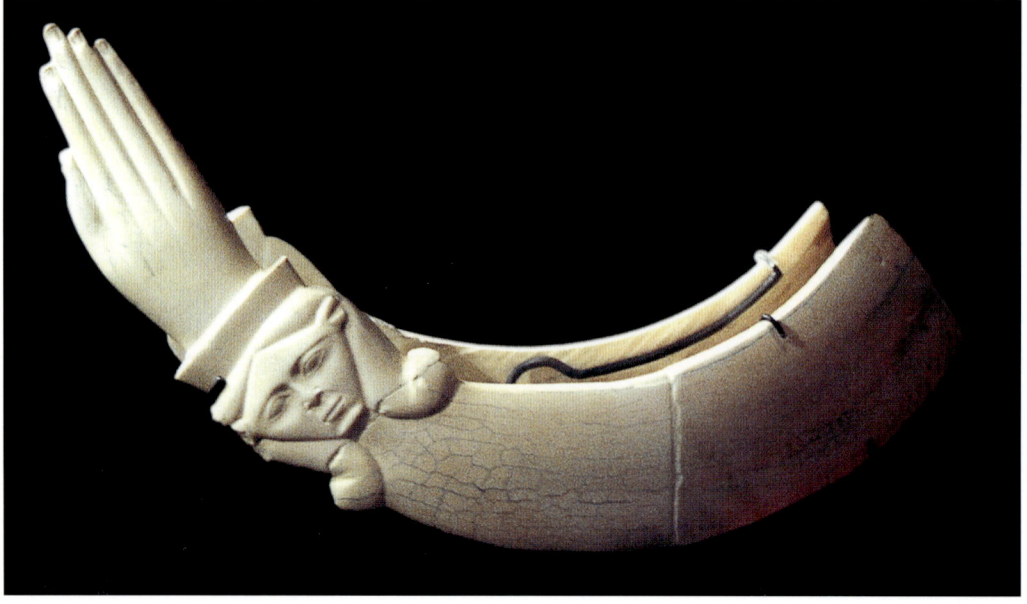

most frequently made of bronze. They were very much associated with the goddess Hathor, whose priestesses shook them as part of the rituals they performed. They often had the head of this goddess incorporated in their design, and they may have been thought to stimulate fertility. In her manifestation as Nebethetepet, or 'Lady of the Vulva', Hathor was represented as a *naos sistrum* (a *sistrum* with the design of a shrine incorporated into it). *Menat*-necklaces were also carried and shaken by the priestesses.

The household spirit-deity, Bes, was often depicted playing various musical instruments, especially a drum or tambourine. Bes was closely associated with pregnancy and childbirth, and music was important in the celebration following a successful birth. Several of the fragments of wall painting found in houses at Deir el-Medina show Bes

▲ *Men and women were never shown dancing together. Here men dance on a relief in the tomb of Kagemni at Saqqara.*

dancing and making music. One fragment reveals a naked, dancing female playing the flute. According to the mythology, Bes appeased the enraged Hathor when she was sulking at Philae by playing the tambourine and harp to her, and he is depicted dancing and playing a tambourine and harp on columns in the Temple of Hathor at Philae.

Births and deaths

In the tale of *The Birth of the Royal Children* on the Middle-Kingdom Papyrus Westcar, the midwives who arrive at the house of the woman in labour are disguised as dancing girls (they also happen to be goddesses). It may well have been common for female dancers to play a part at the time of birth. A scene in the Sixth-Dynasty tomb of Mereruka at Saqqara depicts a female dancing troupe (a *khener*) before his wife Watekhethor, and the hieroglyphic text reads: 'But see the secret of birth! Oh pull!'

Dancers were also present at funerals to elate the spirit of the dead, and to scare away evil spirits. These were the *muu*-dancers who wore kilts and tall, white reed headdresses. From as early as the Fifth Dynasty (c.2490 BC), lion-masked dwarves appear to have been linked to groups of women employed to sing and dance on religious occasions.

Agricultural rites

Singing was a key element of the rites associated with agriculture. Harvesters might chant a lament, accompanied by a flute, in order to express their sorrow at the first cutting of the crops, which was thought to symbolize the wounding of Osiris, the god of vegetation. Dancing was also related to agricultural rites, both as a means of stimulating growth and as

▲ *The ancient Egyptians appear to have made little distinction between dancing and what we would describe as acrobatics, shown in this relief from Hatshepsut's chapel at Karnak.*

a form of thanksgiving. A particularly good example of agricultural dances at the time of the harvest can be found in the Theban tomb of Antefoker dating from the Middle Kingdom (c.2055–1650 BC). The dances appear to be measured and fairly sedate. The *keskes*-dance, associated with Hathor, involved holding mirrors and what appear to be wooden or ivory sticks, carved in the shape of a hand at one end; they were probably clappers. The hand-shaped implements may be linked to Hathor in her aspect of Djeritef, 'his hand', that is the hand of Atum, said in the Heliopolitan creation myth, to have created Shu and Tefnut by masturbating.

A limestone relief of c.1400 BC, now in the British Museum, London, includes a male figure with a lion's head (possibly a Bes mask), carrying a staff with a human hand at the tip, in a register labelled 'dancing by children'. ◆

The Positive Influence of the Dead

The Ancient Egyptians believed that the dead (especially spouses and relatives) possessed supernatural powers that might be called upon to solve various problems in the lives of those still living. The best evidence for this belief comes from the fascinating letters that have survived, written from a living person to a dead one. Today these letters are referred to as Letters to the Dead. The 20 or so that we know of range in date from c.3100–c.1200 BC, but a corresponding oral practice may have been common throughout Egyptian history.

Letters to the Dead

The letters were placed in the tombs of the people to whom they were addressed, probably at the time of the funeral or when the tomb was reopened for later burials. Some were written on pottery dishes, and it is possible that they were left at the tomb full of food offerings, so that as the spirit of the deceased symbolically ate the food the

▶ A continuous supply of food offerings helped ensure the beneficence of the spirits of the deceased. This wooden model of a female offering bearer is from the tomb of Assiut. Middle Kingdom.

text would reveal itself. One such letter, written in ink in hieratic, can be seen on a shallow pottery dish in the Petrie Museum of Egyptian Archaeology in London. It dates to the First Inter-mediate Period (c.2181–c.2055 BC) and was discovered at Diospolis in Upper Egypt. The letter is to the dead man Nefersekhi from his 'sister' (probably his widow making use of a term of affection). She tells him that a trustee of the dead man's property is defrauding their daughter of her share of the inheritance, and she is desperately appealing for his intervention.

The content of this letter is typical – it is addressed to a man (usually it was a deceased husband or father who was appealed to in this way), it deals with legal problems (and especially wrangles over inheritance), and it supposes that now that the man is dead he is closer to the divine world – making it easier for him to influence it – and that he himself now has supernatural powers that could be of use to those still alive.

Another similar example, dating to the Old Kingdom (c.2686–c.2181 BC), can be found on a piece of linen in the Cairo Museum. It is addressed to the deceased

◀ Jewellery and other personal adornment was by no means restricted to women in ancient Egyptian society, as exemplified here by Sennefer's large gold earrings and bracelets in a painting on the wall of his tomb.

head of the family by his widow and son. They are distressed because, against their wishes, relatives have come and removed pottery and servants or slaves from their house. The widow is particularly upset and she says that she would rather that either she or her son died (it is not quite clear which one) than she should see her son subordinated to this rogue branch of the family. The letter begins with the widow reminding the dead husband and father that he himself had spoken out against these thieving members of the family on his deathbed. She and her son quote him on the importance of inheritance and of solidarity between the generations.

It is difficult to be certain exactly how the dead man was expected to help the situation. Perhaps the widow had decided to seek help from her husband after her case had failed in the local court. It seems that the widow thought that her husband might be able to pursue the case in a kind of parallel divine court. It is possible that the piece of linen was originally wrapped around some kind of votive offering to the spirit of the dead man.

A cure for infertility

In addition to helping out with legal problems, deceased relatives were also appealed to when a woman was having difficulties conceiving a child. Because there were no practical measures to cure infertility, and because a woman's ability to have children was so important to her status and well being, both in this life and the next, childless women would seek help from the divine or spirit world. An Old Kingdom Letter to the Dead on a pot now in the Haskell Oriental Museum of Chicago is a plea to a deceased father from his daughter. It reads: 'Cause now that there be born to me a healthy male child. (For) you are an *akh iker* [excellent spirit].'

Fertility figurines have also survived inscribed with a request to a father to grant his daughter a child. These female figurines, with their exaggerated pubic regions, clearly symbolized fertility and sexuality. There seems little reason to attempt a distinction between the possible erotic and procreative connotations of these figures, for as far as the ancient Egyptians were concerned both concepts united to ensure the continued existence of the people of Egypt. The figurines themselves would have served as votive offerings to the dead. One Middle Kingdom example in the Berlin Museum has a child on the left hip, and an inscription on the right thigh reads: 'May a birth be granted to your daughter Seh.' The ancient Egyptians' belief in the creative and magical potency of the written word was profound. In the inscription on this

▲ *In a painting on the wall of his tomb in Aswan, Sarenput sits before a table laden with offerings.*

particular figurine, the quail chick used to write the letter 'w' has been written without legs. Could this have been to safeguard against this hieroglyphic sign coming to life and disappearing? Or perhaps it was intended to reduce the danger such a chick could pose to the crops.

A cure for an illness

The dead were sometimes called upon to help cure illness. The 'Cairo Bowl', which dates to the early Twelfth Dynasty (c.1900 BC), has a letter on it from a woman named Dedi, addressed to her dead husband. It tells him that their servant-girl is ill, and appeals to him to help her to get better.

Ritual objects used in everyday magic, such as apotropaic wands, have been discovered in the accessible outer areas of tombs. They may have been placed there to benefit from the supernatural powers of the dead person. In recent times, village magicians in Egypt and the Sudan are known to have given added power to their magic charms by temporarily burying them in the vicinity of tombs (the most popular tombs being those of people particularly respected in life for their wisdom or piety). Execration figurines have also been found buried near tombs (see *Paraphernalia of Ritual*), perhaps with the intention that the dead would continue the punishment of the enemies of Egypt into the Afterlife. ◆

The Negative Influence of the Dead

The ancient Egyptians believed that unsettled dead people could haunt them and cause them all kinds of distress. These were the spirits of people who had died violently or too young or without a proper burial, or they might have failed to achieve what was expected of them in life, such as the production of children. If an inexplicable disaster struck an Egyptian family, such as a severe illness or the sudden loss of livestock, then a dead person's spirit might be behind it. To forestall such losses and afflictions at the hands of the dead, it was thought a sensible precaution to propitiate their spirits with regular offerings, and to do nothing that might offend them. At all times it was considered that the dead required respect from their families and descendants.

In one story that is partly preserved on several ostraca of the late second millennium BC, the High Priest of Amun-Re confronts an *akh* ('spirit')

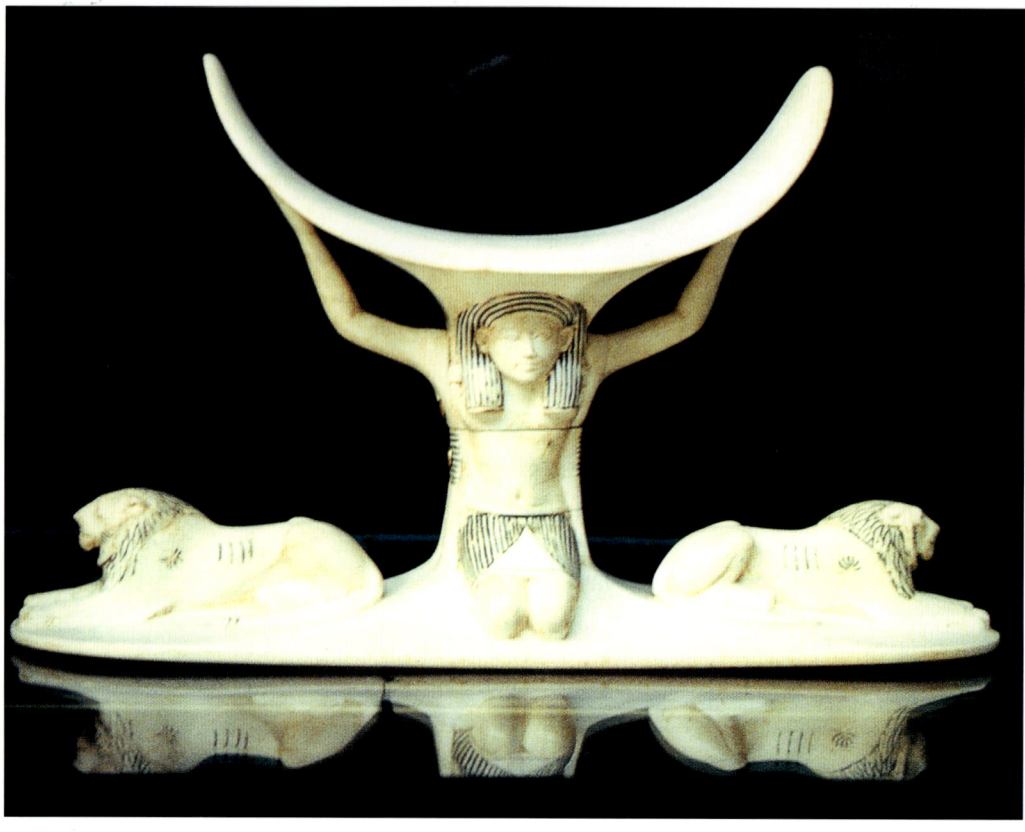

▲ *The recumbent lions on Tutankhamun's headrest were intended to protect the sleeper. Funerary art often shows the crouching lion serving a defensive role.*

Exorcism

The curses known as the Execration Texts were mainly aimed at the destruction of Egypt's enemies, but some were written to exorcise the malignant ghosts of those who had rebelled against the state. By destroying the names of these people, their spirits were considered to have been vanquished, thereby extending their punishment into the Afterlife.

The defacement of images of the dead person also amounted to an attack on his or her spirit in the Afterlife. If the tomb was destroyed, it followed that the spirit would no longer be able to receive sustaining offerings and its power would be correspondingly diminished or eliminated.

who has been causing trouble in the Theban necropolis. The ghost admits that it is unhappy because its tomb has fallen into disrepair. In an attempt to settle and appease this restless spirit, the High Priest promises an endowment for cult offerings and a whole new tomb. The ancient Egyptians believed that food offerings and the preservation of the body were crucial for a contented existence in the Afterlife.

Troublesome women

Whereas it was usual to invoke dead husbands and fathers for help and guidance, it tended to be the spirits of dead women who were regarded as troublemakers. In a Letter to the Dead on papyrus which is now in the Rijksmuseum van Oudheden in Leiden, a widowed husband living in Memphis during the Nineteenth Dynasty writes to his wife, who seems to have been dead for about two years. He makes it quite clear that he cared for her during her lifetime and that he has stayed faithful to her after death, and so he does not think it is fair that she should continue to haunt him. Sadly, the letter does not tell us how the hauntings were manifesting themselves, but the man in question had quite clearly had enough and he threatens his deceased wife with some kind of court case before a divine tribunal. A similar letter was written on an ostracon dating to the end of the Twentieth Dynasty, from the Scribe of the Necropolis, Butehamon, to his dead wife Akhtai.

Protection against ghosts

Female ghosts were considered a particular threat to pregnant women and nursing mothers, and to young children, especially if the ghost's antecedent had

▲ *A small pyramidion marked the tomb chapels of the New Kingdom rock-cut tombs at Deir el-Medina, such as this one belonging to the craftsman of the royal tomb, Amennakht, and his wife Nubemsha.*

died before giving birth successfully herself. Many of the oracular amuletic decrees, and the texts in the Brooklyn Magical Papyrus dating to the first millennium BC, mention female ghosts as a dangerous threat against which precautions must be taken.

Another type of harmful spirit was referred to as *mut*, which is often translated as 'dangerous dead'. The texts sometimes classify executed traitors and prisoners of war as *mut*. But in everyday magic, a *mut* seems to have been a ghost who could or would not pass on to the realm of the dead and therefore continued to plague the living.

The ancient Egyptians also used spells to protect themselves against terrifying night-time apparitions (of both male and female ghosts). It was believed that the dead could cause nightmares, and even inflict sickness on the sleeper. In addition to spells to guard against these, they used headrests decorated with apotropaic figures to ward off evil, such as those of the protective household deities Bes and Taweret.

The magico-medical texts quite often cite the malign influence of the dead as a cause of disease, or as a threat to its cure. Even the shadow of a dead person was regarded as a potential source of harm to the medicine prepared by a doctor. Spells were devised to drive the dead out of the limbs of a patient.

Even otherwise benign spirits were considered to be capable of punishing the living if they were roused. The degree of violence that the dead were credited with is exemplified by those tomb inscriptions that warned anyone thinking of robbing the tomb that the dead person was now capable of exacting revenge by killing the robber and ruining his whole family. ◆

Temples and Priests

The temples of ancient Egypt have inspired awe throughout the ages. The modern visitor still marvels at their magnificence – their huge size and the beauty and detail of the reliefs on their walls.

To ensure their survival, these grand structures, mostly of stone, were built in the desert fringes, just beyond the reaches of the Nile flood. It is, of course, the most recent structure at any one site that still stands today, and most surviving temples are not pharaonic at all, but date to the Ptolemaic and Roman Periods (332 BC–AD 395). They do, however, comply with the ancient conventions of temple-building. It was possible for a cult centre to have been dedicated to a particular deity for centuries, while the temple itself was rebuilt, perhaps more than once.

The architectural splendour of the great religious buildings is impossible to overlook, but finding out what actually went on inside them involves closer scrutiny. As well as inscriptions on temple walls, hymns, prayers and records of administration and offerings were kept on papyri. Many votive offerings have also survived. From such sources it is possible to build up a picture of the roles of the various priests, and to begin to fathom the rituals of the High Priest, who enjoyed a more intimate interaction with the resident deity of the temple.

◀ *Colossal statues of rulers and elaborately decorated columns were key features of the great temples of Egypt.*

Temple Architecture

The temples that survive in Egypt today tend to date from the New Kingdom onwards (c.1550 BC). They may have varied in size depending on the importance of a particular deity, but whether they were dedicated to gods or kings (living or dead), all Egyptian temples had essential architectural features in common.

The grand approach

Each temple was approached by a processional way or avenue, often flanked by rows of statues. The approach to Karnak Temple is typical, lined on each side by stone sphinxes with ram's heads (the ram was one of the guises of Amun, who was worshipped at this temple). It once connected the great complex at Karnak with Luxor Temple, about 2km (1 mile) to the south.

The processional way led to the main gateway, known as the first pylon (the ancient Greek word for 'gate') of the temple. This consisted of two enormous tapering towers of masonry with an opening between them. Flags on long poles projected outwards from the front of the temple on each side of the entrance. These flags, flying majestically, would have been visible from a long way off and would have been an image closely associated with the temple. It is therefore interesting that the hieroglyphic sign used to write the ancient Egyptian word *netjer*, which means 'god', was possibly intended to represent a flag on a pole. The onlooker would also have been struck by the size of the statues of the king which flanked the gateway, such as those of Ramesses II (c.1279–c.1213 BC) at Luxor Temple. It would certainly have heightened the people's belief in the divinity of kingship to witness these statues of the ruler in such a hallowed setting, and being so colossal they must have seemed like gods. Sometimes an obelisk, or a pair of obelisks, also marked the entrance to the temple.

▲ *There were originally two obelisks in front of the First Pylon at Luxor Temple, but the other is now in the Place de la Concorde in Paris.*

▼ *The roof of the great hypostyle hall at Karnak Temple was originally supported by 134 massive stone columns.*

▶ *Plant-life is a common theme of temple decoration, and is seen here at Kom Ombo.*

Inside the great entrance was the peristyle court, a large, open square surrounded by a colonnade. It is likely that some of the population (at least in the later periods of Egyptian history) would have been allowed at certain times into this 'public' area of the temple, although all who entered the temple's confines would have had to comply with the criteria of ritual purity (see *The Temple Complex*).

The temple lay on a straight axis. On the other side of the great court, opposite the back of the first pylon, was a smaller gateway known as the second pylon. Access through this inner entrance was restricted to those with priestly titles, and the rooms within were used for storing cult equipment and for performing the secret rituals of the temple (see *Temple Rites and Offerings*).

The inner sanctum
On the other side of the second pylon was the hypostyle hall, with a roof supported by rows of columns. This was usually broader than it was deep. To walk through it was like wandering through a forest. Gaps at the top of the outer walls provided clerestory lighting – shafts of light piercing the mysterious darkness. It would have been only just possible to make out the painted reliefs and inscriptions on the walls and columns. The gloom and the dense columns formed a perfect screen between the outside world and the secluded dwelling-place of the god.

The number of peristyle courts and hypostyle halls depended on the size of the temple, as did the number of storerooms, antechambers, vestibules, offering halls and shrines which led off the inner hypostyle hall. But deep within every temple lay the 'holy of holies' – the sanctuary where the god lived. The

god or goddess resided in a cult statue, which stood in a raised shrine or *naos* (the ancient Greek word for the innermost part of a temple or shrine), usually of stone or wood with wooden doors. From the New Kingdom onwards (c.1550 BC) the shrine often took the form of a boat, as at the temple of Horus at Edfu, and was known as a barque shrine. Only the High Priest could enter the presence of the god.

The god's home
The temple was very much the house of the god. The ancient Egyptian for 'temple' was *hwt netjer*, 'the god's mansion', or *per netjer*, 'the god's house'. The temple was also regarded as a model of the place where creation was believed to have taken place. The floor level rose gradually from the temple entrance to the shrine in the innermost sanctuary, and the *naos* was thought to reflect the mound projecting from the primordial waters, with the deity standing on it as the creator god had first done.

The primordial waters (Nun) were symbolized by a 'sacred lake', such as at Karnak, where the priests made their ablutions. The Victory Stela of Piy (c.747–c.716 BC) in the Cairo Museum records that when this Twenty-fifth-Dynasty king visited Heliopolis and ritually cleansed himself in the sacred lake there, he claimed that he had washed his face in 'the river of Nun', as the sun god was believed to do each day before dawn. It is also possible that the

undulating mudbrick wall surrounding some of the temple enclosures was meant to represent the waters of chaos.

The cosmological theme was extended elsewhere inside the temple. A marsh was evoked by the halls with their rows of papyrus- and lotus-form columns. The flat ceilings were often painted dark blue and covered with yellow stars. The hieroglyphic sign for 'horizon' was a tract of land with the sun rising between two mountains, and it is possible that the great pylon forming the entrance to the temple was meant to represent this. ◆

▲ *The monolithic* naos *of highly polished syenite in the sanctuary at Edfu Temple is the oldest part of the building, dating to the 30th-Dynasty reign of Nectanebo II.*

Different Types of Temples

There were two main types of temple: cult temples dedicated to deities, and mortuary temples built in honour of dead kings. Both were very similar in design and function: offerings were made to the gods in the former, to ensure the beneficence of the divine world; and to the spirits (*kas*) of the deceased kings in the latter, ensuring their continued existence in the Afterlife. Both procedures were seen as crucial to the maintenance of order and peace (see *Temple Rites and Offerings*).

Cult temples were usually dedicated to a triad of deities, whereas mortuary temples were concerned with the deceased king and his identification with a number of gods. A king's mortuary temple was clearly also intended to be used for ceremonies during his lifetime, and provided the focal point for a complex of buildings built in celebration of divine kingship, including a royal palace which could go

▲ *The columns in this colonnade at Karnak are papyriform: their capitals resemble stylized papyrus buds.*

on to serve as a dummy palace for the dead king's spirit.

In all temples, priests officiated (see *The Role of Priests*), offerings were made and rituals performed. The focal point of any cult temple was the statue of a god, whereas in a royal mortuary temple it was the statue of a king.

Cult temples

Very little has survived of cult temples built before the New Kingdom (c.1550 BC). During the Old Kingdom (c.2686–c.2181 BC) it is likely that temples to the deities were built of mudbrick, which is obviously a less durable building material than stone. (Today, Egyptian farmers make use of the ancient mudbrick as a fertilizer, called *sebakh* in Arabic.) During the Middle Kingdom (c.2055–c.1650 BC) cult temples were apparently built of stone, but little has survived. Usually the stone from these structures was re-used in the buildings of the New Kingdom (c.1550–c.1069 BC) and later temples located on the same sites as the earlier ones. The ancient Egyptians were great recyclers, as modern Egyptians are today. Why go

to the bother of quarrying in the searing heat of the desert, transporting heavy loads across vast distances and working stone with stone and bronze tools, when ready-dressed blocks were available on the site from an earlier structure that had perhaps fallen into disrepair? A good example of such re-use is a stunning relief of the Twelfth-Dynasty king Senusret I (c.1965–c.1920 BC) and the god Min which presumably once graced the walls of an important Middle Kingdom temple. Now in the Petrie Museum of Egyptian Archaeology, it was discovered by the 'Father of Egyptian archaeology', William Matthew Flinders Petrie (1853–1942), turned face down and re-used as a paving slab in a much later Ptolemaic temple at the site of Koptos.

Mortuary temples

Royal mortuary temples (referred to in the ancient texts as 'mansions of millions of years') have survived from

▲ *Statues of Ramesses II in the form of Osiris stand before pillars in this king's mortuary temple, the Ramesseum.*

the Early Dynastic Period onwards (c.3100 BC). They became larger and grander as time went on. The earliest examples are simple offering chambers adjoining the earliest royal tombs, called mastabas (Arabic for 'bench') at the royal burial sites of Abydos and Saqqara. By the Third Dynasty they were more complex. The mortuary temple in the burial complex of King Djoser (c.2667–c.2648 BC) was attached to the north face of his pyramid. It was made of stone and consisted of two courts, one of which was presumably dedicated to Djoser as king of Upper Egypt, and one to him as king of Lower Egypt. By the Fourth Dynasty, the mortuary temple had been shifted to the east face of the pyramid, so that it could be joined via a straight causeway to a 'valley temple' at the edge of the cultivation, usually at a quay on a canal. The best preserved mortuary temples from the Old Kingdom (c.2686–c.2181

▼ *The unusual altar in the sun temple of Niuserre at Abu Gurab is sculpted out of calcite and is some 6m (20ft) in diameter. 5th Dynasty.*

BC) are those of king Khafre (c.2558–c.2532 BC) at Giza.

By the New Kingdom (c.1550–c.1069 BC), the mortuary temples were separate from the tombs of the kings. The tombs were in the Valley of the Kings on the west bank at Thebes, whereas their accompanying temples were some distance away on the desert fringes, more conveniently sited close to the cultivation and the river. They were imposing structures, elaborately decorated and on a par with the contemporary state cult temples.

A variation on the theme of the mortuary temple were the 'cenotaph temples' at Abydos, the legendary burial

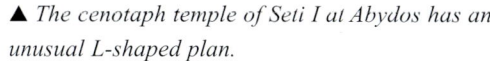
▲ *The cenotaph temple of Seti I at Abydos has an unusual L-shaped plan.*

place of Osiris, god of the dead, rebirth and vegetation. These temples were closely associated with the cult of Osiris, and their function was to associate the dead king with various gods. The earliest royal cenotaph at Abydos was built by the Twelfth-Dynasty king Senusret III (c.1874–c.1855 BC), but by far the best preserved and thus best known is that of the Nineteenth-Dynasty ruler Seti I (c.1294–c.1279 BC).

Sun temples

The remains of stone sun temples date from the Fifth Dynasty (c.2494–c.2345 BC). They were dedicated to the sun god Re, but were also closely associated with royal burials. They were built by the first six rulers of this dynasty and were connected with their pyramids (which, like the obelisk, were presumably solar symbols) and with the cult of the sun god at Heliopolis. Six sun temples are known from inscriptions, but only two have actually been discovered; they are those of Userkaf (c.2494–c.2487 BC) and Niuserre (c.2445–c.2421 BC), and are both situated at Abu Gurab, north of Abusir (part of the necropolis of ancient Memphis). The sun temple of Niuserre houses the remains of an enormous squat stone obelisk, and a gigantic altar in the form of four hieroglyphic signs for 'offering' (*hetep*). ◆

The Temple Complex

The purpose of the ancient Egyptian temple was to reflect and maintain the divine order of creation. It was not a place of organized public worship, comparable with a mosque, synagogue or church. No form of service was held, and rather than everyone being welcomed into the temple, the public were generally excluded from it. A large number of priests was employed by each temple but very few of them actually performed religious rituals.

The temple was rather like a medieval European monastery, in that it was a great landowning institution and functioned very much as the hub of the local economy, and as a place of learning. It was run by a large and complex bureaucracy, and temple workers included farmers, builders and scribes as well as priests.

▲ *The ears on this painted stela were included to ensure that the god would hear the prayer.*

Ritual purity

All who entered the confines of the temple had to comply with the strict rules regarding ritual purity. According to inscriptions on the walls of the temple at Esna, all those entering temples from the Late Period (c.747 BC) were expected at least to have cut their fingernails and toenails, shaved their heads and removed other body hair, washed their hands with natron (a naturally occurring salt), be dressed in linen (they were forbidden from wearing wool), and to have not had sexual intercourse for several days. Priests were not required to remain celibate outside the temple.

Much ritual purification would subsequently have gone on inside the temple, making use of ablution tanks and the Sacred Lake.

Public access to the deity

During much of Egyptian history most people would have been allowed only as far as the gateway of the temple complex. They did, however, come to the outer precincts of the temple to say prayers and enlist the help of the gods. At the mortuary temple of Ramesses III (c.1184–c.1153 BC) at Medinet Habu, for example, the corridor inside the entrance gateway had an image of 'Ptah who hears prayers' on its wall. In this way, people who would only ever be granted access to this part of the temple could petition, or give thanks to, the god. No member of the public would ever have laid eyes on the cult statue of the god housed in the inner shrine. However, by the later period of Egyptian history, the peristyle court (see *Temple Architecture*) appears to have become available to a certain degree of public access, and was a place where offerings and supplications could be made before statues of gods and kings (see *Temple Rites and Offerings*). The emphasis was on the gods hearing the prayers of the people, so stelae, statues and even walls might be inscribed with numerous ears in order to ensure this would happen. Sometimes stelae and statues set up in the outer parts of the temple were covered in hieroglyphs. These were often spells to help to cure, or protect against, scorpion stings, snake bites, and other such hazards and illnesses.

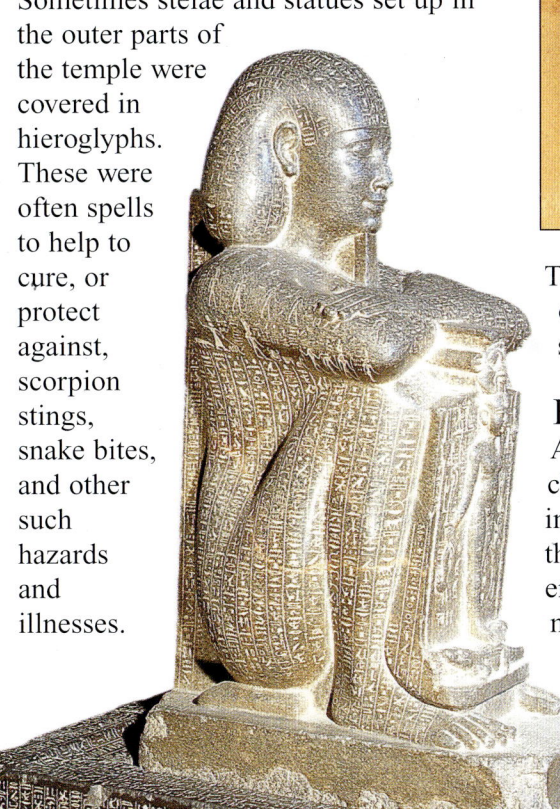

Today these stelae are known as *cippi* of Horus and the statues as 'healing statues'.

▲ *Musical instruments of all kinds were played in the temples. Paintings and reliefs reveal that male harpists were often blind. 18th Dynasty. Tomb of Nakht, west Thebes.*

Festivals

At all times of the year singing, chanting and the playing of musical instruments would have taken place in the temples – the gods were thought to enjoy such aural delights at all times, but never more so than at the festivals, the most joyous occasions in the lives of the temples. It was at these celebrations that the statue of the deity emerged from his or her secluded shrine, carried on the shoulders of priests, but always still concealed from the eyes of the masses, sometimes in a carrying shrine in the form of a boat (known as a barque shrine). The oracle of the god could then be consulted. His or her answer might be sought to questions such as whether it was sensible to make a difficult journey north, or who, out of a list of suspects, was responsible for stealing an article of clothing.

◄ *This basalt 'healing statue' of the priest Djedhor is covered in hieroglyphs of incantatory texts. The priest sits behind a* cippus *of Horus, and the basin in the plinth is for the collection of water which was ritually poured over the statue to be imbued with the potency of the magic spells. 30th Dynasty.*

▲ *The foreleg of the ox was the choice cut of meat for offering to the gods and to the dead. 6th Dynasty. Tomb of Idut, Saqqara.*

The god's needs

The daily rituals of the temple took place in the darker, more secluded parts of the building on the far side of the hypostyle hall (see *Temple Architecture* and *Temple Rites and Offerings*). Every need of the deity was tended to, directly by a minority of the priesthood and indirectly by a large number of temple workers. According to the longest known papyrus from ancient Egypt, Papyrus Harris (40.5m or 133ft long), which dates to the day the Twentieth-Dynasty king Ramesses III died

▶ *The migdol gateway of Ramesses III's mortuary temple at Medinet Habu was a quasi-defensive feature borrowed from the design of Syrian fortresses.*

▲ *Windows in the inner parts of temples were usually clerestory, allowing shafts of light to filter down from the tops of the walls, as here in the hypostyle hall at Edfu.*

(c.1153 BC), the estate of Karnak Temple employed a total labour force of 81,322 people (see *The Role of Priests*). The papyrus also records that this great temple of Amun exercised control over 2393sq km (924sq miles) of arable land, 433 orchards, 421,362 head of livestock, 65 villages, 83 ships and 46 workshops.

Temple economy

The ancient Egyptian temple was the economic hub of the locality. The temple complex would have had its own landing quay, giving it easy access to the river for transporting produce. In the larger temple complexes, food production would have taken place on a grand scale in the temple butcheries, breweries and bakeries.

By a process known as the 'reversion of offerings', a large proportion of the population could in practice be fed via the temple. Much of the produce of Egypt passed, by various requirements, to the temples throughout the country, especially in the big cities such as Thebes and Memphis where there were huge temple complexes, each with a number of different deities to be offered to on a daily basis. The greater the quantity of offerings, it was hoped, the greater the beneficence of the gods. Food offerings of all kinds were made to the gods, but most of what was offered eventually reverted to the priests. From them it was passed to their families and to the many workers and dependents of the temple and temple estates, not to mention the poor at the temple gate (see *Temple Rites and Offerings*).

A place of scholarship

The temple was also a place of learning, providing education for those boys who would go on to hold administrative or priestly positions. During the New Kingdom (c.1550–c.1069 BC), it is known from texts that there were at least two schools in Thebes, one in the temple of the goddess Mut at Karnak, and one behind the Ramesseum, the mortuary complex of the Nineteenth-Dynasty king Ramesses II (c.1279–c.1213 BC), although no excavated structure has been found which can be identified as having been used as a school.

The local temple was the storehouse for local records, which were written on papyrus rolls kept in locked chests. In general, the temple, with its high surrounding walls and massive gateway, would have functioned as the local safe place. The temple at Medinet Habu, for instance, was one of the most defensible places in western Thebes. The east gate was fortified with guardhouses flanking the entrance, and in the late Twentieth Dynasty, when the people of the west Theban workmen's village of Deir el-Medina felt threatened by marauding foreigners, they hid themselves in the precincts of the temple. ◆

The Role of Priests

If, as is stated in Papyrus Harris (c.1153 BC), the temple of Amun at Karnak employed 81,322 people towards the end of the New Kingdom, it is clear that the temples must have been the chief places of employment in the country. There is no implication that those 81,322 individuals could possibly all have been priests. In fact it is a matter of dispute whether any of these temple employees would actually have been priests in the modern sense of the term.

The conventional translations of ancient Egyptian terms can be misleading when they employ words that have very specific meanings and associations for us today. The ancient Egyptian term *hem netjer* is normally translated as 'priest', but it literally means 'servant of the god' and not all those described in this way were necessarily trained in theology. They certainly would not have conducted the kind of worship or services performed by priests in any of the religious traditions that are familiar today. It is possible that most of those described as 'servants of the god' would not have performed any kind of ritual in the temple.

Priestly garments

Apart from the obligation to be clean shaven, priests of lower ranks who are depicted in reliefs and paintings are indistinguishable from ordinary people. However, some priests did wear distinctive clothing as a sign of their office. The *sem-*priests who performed the final purification and revivification rites at funerals, wore cloaks made of leopardskin. When the king was portrayed officiating in his priestly role he was sometimes shown wearing this form of dress.

▲ *Tuthmosis III wears a leopardskin to identify his role as High Priest.*

A priestly rota

The number of temple employees depended on the size of the temple, which in turn depended on the status of the deity to whom it was dedicated and the size of the town or city. Throughout Egyptian history, the main body of priests was made up of people who spent much of the year engaged in their own, different, occupations. A rota system was devised whereby the priests of each temple were divided into four groups (usually referred to today by the Greek word *phyle*). The members of each group performed their temple

▲ *A libation of water (indicated by a zig-zag line, the hieroglyphic sign for water) is poured from a heset-jar on to a heaped offering table in this relief at the temple of Kom Ombo.*

▼ *An enormous variety of foods, including beef, fish, duck, bread, fruit and vegetables, were offered to the gods and to the spirits of the dead. Tomb of Horemheb, Saqqara.*

duties for one month, then returned to their own jobs for three months, so that they worked for the temple for a total of three months in every year. At the end of each month-long shift, a stock taking was carried out, and records were made on papyri or wooden boards.

For most members of the community, it would have been well worth their while to perform this temple service because the priests received a proportion of the temple revenue (this would have been given in kind, because there was no coinage in ancient Egypt). The ancient Egyptians believed that the deity consumed the essence of the food given to him or her as an offering, and it could then be passed on to the priests. This system was known as the 'reversion of offerings' (see *The Temple Complex*). The practice could at times prove lucrative – as it did during the New Kingdom (c.1550–c.1069 BC) when tithes and war booty created huge temple incomes – to the extent that it was sometimes even considered worth purchasing a priestly office.

Priests were also exempted from some taxes, and could often avoid undertaking state labour that was otherwise a compulsory service, such as the digging of irrigation systems.

The purified ones

Most of the priests had very little contact with the cult statue of the deity, the focal point of any temple, although tending the statue was the most important temple rite and would have been carried out by the most senior priests. The reliefs on temple walls can be misleading because it was believed that it was only the king who was worthy of being depicted standing opposite a deity, so priests are never shown making offerings to the gods.

All those working in the temple had to be considered ritually pure in order to do so. In fact the majority of the priests

▲ *The calendars of festivals carved on the walls of temples such as this one at Kom Ombo, were based on the lunar months, stellar sightings and the annual inundation of the Nile.*

◄ *The 18th-Dynasty king Ay (c.1327– c.1323 BC) is depicted on the north wall of Tutankhamun's burial chamber wearing the leopardskin of a priest and performing the ritual of the Opening of the Mouth on the mummy of the dead king; thus Ay legitimized his accession to the throne as Tutankhamun's heir.*

were called *wab* ('purifier' or 'purified') priests. The Greek historian Herodotus, writing in the fifth century BC, stated that Egyptian priests washed twice daily and twice nightly, that they were clean-shaven, had no body hair, were circumcised, abstained from sexual intercourse for several days before entering the temple, wore no wool or leather clothing, and had sandals made of papyrus. In addition, priests seem to have had to rinse out their mouths with a solution of natron (a natural compound of sodium carbonate and bicarbonate, found as crystals at the edges of certain lakes) and rub their bodies with oil.

A judicial document now in the Turin Museum tells us that a *wab* priest of Khnum was brought to justice because he had sworn not to enter the temple at Elephantine until he had spent ten days drinking natron, but in fact he had entered after only seven days and was considered ritually impure.

A variety of jobs

Most priests would not have come into direct contact with the divine cult image, so although their job might have been to see

to the needs of the god, it would have been only by indirect means. The man who was able to interact most closely with the god was the High Priest (see *The High Priests*). His deputy was the Second Prophet, who was in charge of the economic organization of the temple. He oversaw its provisioning from estates and endowments, and he made sure that the right amount of offerings were delivered each day. He would have had a host of administrators working with him.

The majority of the priests were occupied with ensuring the maintenance and security of the temple. They ran the workshops, storerooms, libraries and other affiliated buildings, as well as acting as doorkeepers and porters. The daily tasks of washing, dressing and feeding the cult statue of the deity appear to have been carried out by Stolist Priests (see *Temple Rites and Offerings*). They would have worked closely with the Lector Priests, whose job it was to recite the words of the god. They chanted magic spells while important rituals were

Special skills

Many priests with specialist knowledge worked in the temples. Examples include the Hour Priests, who were perhaps astronomers responsible for compiling the calendars of festivals – occasions when the priests carried the cult statue of the deity into the local community, and manipulated the divine oracle. Scholarly priests, who worked in the House of Life (*Per Ankh*), taught reading and writing to the elite local boys, and copied out manuscripts for the temple library or record office. Many of them would have functioned as scribes in the local community, being called upon to write up documents such as wills or divorce settlements. Some priests were considered able to interpret dreams, and thereby provide a form of guidance and prophesy. Others would have been cult singers and temple musicians.

carried out; for example, they would recite spells from the Book of the Dead while a dead body was being embalmed and mummified.

The *sem*-priest, who can be distinguished in images by the leopardskin he wears, was also very important at death. This priest's function developed in the New Kingdom out of the duties performed by the first-born son at his father's funeral. These included the final rites of purification and the Opening of the Mouth ceremony, which was performed on the mummified body to revive its senses, so that the deceased could be reborn.

All those people who worked in the temple confines had to swear not to spread the secrets or mysteries of the temple, and were considered to occupy a privileged position. ◆

◀ *This priest has a figure of the god Amun tattooed on his upper arm. He kneels behind an image of the god. As is often the case, an inscription accompanies the statue.*

The High Priests

The king was nominally High Priest of every cult in Egypt, but basic logistics clearly prevented him from performing the daily rituals in many places at once, and so in practice he had to delegate the day-to-day duties of High Priest to men stationed at temples throughout the country. Thus the position of High Priest (or Chief Priest or First Prophet) was by royal appointment and was a highly esteemed title, both religiously and politically.

Acting on behalf of the king, the High Priest had closer contact with the cult statue of the god than anyone else in the temple complex. It is likely that only the High Priest would have been allowed to stand before the image of the god in the shrine. Temple reliefs illustrate what was expected of the High Priest, but because the presence of the king was still considered necessary in the temples, even if only symbolically, it was the ruler who was shown performing the rituals in the various reliefs and statuary (see *Temple Rites and Offerings*). Superb reliefs on the walls of the sanctuaries in the temple at Abydos, for example, depict the Nineteenth-Dynasty king Seti I (c.1294–c.1279 BC) carrying out his priestly duties.

Nepotism

In the Old Kingdom (c.2686–c.2181 BC) all senior positions, whether in the temples, the administrative system or the army, were held by the same small group of people, more specifically members of the royal family – especially brothers, sons and uncles of the reigning monarch – who held multiple honorary titles, each accompanied by privileges granted by the king. As priests these men would certainly have played a role in the temple structure, but would probably not have worked full-time within the temple confines. During the Middle Kingdom (c.2055–c.1650 BC) these three sources of employment for the élite became more distinct, but the highest ranking priests continued also to sit on councils of state in the royal palace, and clearly they had political influence.

▲ *The leopardskin was a priestly robe usually associated with the sem-priest.*

During the Eighteenth Dynasty (c.1550–c.1295 BC) the wealth of the largest temples grew dramatically, mainly augmented by booty and tribute resulting from successful military campaigning in Syria-Palestine. The Temple of Amun at Karnak received the bulk of this new source of income, and its High Priest became more and more powerful, thanks to the wealth and manpower under his control. According to Papyrus Harris, by the end of Ramesses III's reign (c.1153 BC) the king had relinquished control over the finances of the estate of Amun. The Wilbour Papyrus, dating to the reign of Ramesses V (c.1147–c.1143 BC), records that this land was not subject to royal taxation, and that its dependants

▲ *The ruler Hatshepsut wears a false beard, the* nemes *headdress – a striped linen headcloth – and a* uraeus *on her brow. She holds two* nw *pots, characteristically used for offering wine and milk to the gods. 18th Dynasty.*

▲ *In the cenotaph temple of Seti I at Abydos, the king burns incense before a seated figure of Horus. The god holds an* ankh *in his left hand and a crook, flail and* was-*sceptre in his right.*

were exempt from compulsory military service and state labour.

Priestly power

If the reigning king was strong and successful, the excessive power of the High Priest of Amun at Karnak did not necessarily cause any real problems. But if a weak and ineffective king succeeded to the throne there was likely to be trouble, and this is exactly what happened towards the end of the Twentieth Dynasty (c.1186– c.1069 BC). Because of the exceptionally long reign of Ramesses II (c.1279–c.1213 BC), many of the last kings of the New Kingdom succeeded to the throne when they were already elderly and feeble. They chose to pass their days in their palace at Per-Ramesses in the Delta, thus distancing themselves from their people and, more significantly, from the Theban region.

Generally their reigns appear to have been fairly ineffectual. But the people of the south of Egypt needed a strong leader, and rather than look to the king they decided it would be most sensible to show allegiance to the High Priest of Amun at Thebes.

At the end of the Twentieth Dynasty, a High Priest of Amun named Herihor was able to get away with claiming royal titles even though Ramesses XI (c.1099– c.1069 BC) was still on the throne. There are inscriptions in the Temple of Khonsu at Karnak which show Herihor's name written in royal cartouches, and his adoption of the full regal titles, including the royal epithet 'Victorious Bull', the rare title 'Great Ruler of Egypt' and even 'Son of Amun', thereby claiming divine descent. This High Priest was militarily and economically incredibly powerful, and during Ramesses XI's reign he effectively controlled Egypt from its southern border at Aswan north to Herakleopolis near the Faiyum. Despite this, at no time did Herihor claim complete royal power. ◆

▲ *It was unheard of for a high priest to have himself represented with royal titles and his name in cartouches, face-to-face with the god Amun, until Herihor brazenly usurped these royal prerogatives here at Karnak.*

The Role of Women in the Temples

◄ *The design of the hooped* sistrum, *or ceremonial rattle, often incorporated the face of Hathor with her cow ears. Tomb of Sennefer.*

and Pakhet, and during the Old Kingdom a certain queen Meresankh held the office of High Priestess of the god Thoth.

Music and dance

An important part of the cult of Hathor was music and dance – the priestesses accompanied ceremonial dances and rituals by shaking their *sistra* (rattles), instruments whose handles were often decorated with the carved head of Hathor, and rattling their broad, beaded necklaces with long counterpoises, called *menat* necklaces.

From the Old Kingdom onwards, women often functioned as the cult singers, dancers and musicians, playing instruments such as harps, tambourines and clappers in the temples of both

► *Amenirdis, the daughter of the Kushite ruler Kashta, was adopted as 'God's Wife of Amun' at Thebes.*

There were far fewer women than men working in the temples of ancient Egypt, but the title 'priestess' (*hemet netjer*, literally 'wife of the god') certainly existed. These women, who functioned in the temple cults, tended to be from the upper echelons of society and were usually married to priests, and as a result their position relied heavily upon the status of their husbands. During the Old and Middle Kingdoms (c.2686–c.1650 BC), the title *hemet netjer* was most usually associated with the cult of Hathor, the goddess of fertility. It was a priestess who was in charge of the management of the estates of this goddess, and even some of the High Priests were women. We also know of female High Priests serving the cults of the goddesses Neith

▲ *This painted limestone stela depicts Nefretiabet seated before an offering table laden with bread and surrounded by other commodities such as oil, incense and meat. A list of types of linen appears on the right. 4th Dynasty.*

The Chief Concubine

The Ramesside sources tell us that the wife of the High Priest of Amun-Re at Karnak held the title 'Chief Concubine of Amun-Re'. She had ritual responsibilities, such as leading the female musicians of the temple, and seems to have wielded a certain amount of power. One record mentions that the Chief Concubine acted to ensure the prompt delivery of overdue rations to the protesting necropolis workers of Deir el-Medina. On another occasion a Chief Concubine arranged for the murder of a troublesome policeman.

gods and goddesses. By the beginning of the New Kingdom (c.1550 BC) the title 'Chantress of Amun' was in fairly common use – once again it was usually the wives of priests who gained positions of this kind.

Funerals

Women played an important role at funerals and, during the Old Kingdom (c.2686–c.2181 BC), in the rituals of the mortuary cults of the deceased. It was common practice for two of the female mourners to take the titles 'Great Kite' and 'Little Kite' and impersonate the goddesses Isis and Nephthys. According to the myth of Osiris, these goddesses had taken the guise of kites as they pieced together the body of the god in order to mummify him. At least during the Old Kingdom, priestesses could hold the title '*Ka*-servant' (*hemet-ka*) and it was their responsibility to perform rituals in the tomb-chapels of the deceased.

The most prestigious religious title held by a woman was 'God's Wife of Amun', which was also, from the Eighteenth Dynasty, a position of great political significance. This office was based at Thebes, and was held by a daughter of the king in order to ensure royal control of the Theban area. From the reign of the Twenty-third Dynasty king Osorkon III (c.777–c.749 BC), the 'God's Wife of Amun' was expected to remain celibate, so she had to adopt a daughter and successor. She was also given the second title 'Hand of the God', possibly giving her a symbolic role in the act of creation. According to one version of the creation myth of Heliopolis, the god Atum had brought the gods Shu and Tefnut into existence by masturbating.

By the Late Period the God's Wife was more important than the High Priest. She controlled the vast estates of Amun, employed huge numbers of people, and had access to great wealth. ◆

Temple Rites and Offerings

Temple rites revolved around the cult statue of the deity, which resided in each temple shrine. We can guess that these cult statues would often have been made of precious materials such as gold and silver, because very few have survived to this day, at least not in situ. Each statue was believed to house the very essence of the deity in question. A ritual ceremony known as the Opening of the Mouth had been performed on every statue in order to animate it symbolically. As a result, the god, together with his or her family, was believed to live in the temple which was regarded as his or her house (*hwt netjer*, 'the god's mansion' or *per netjer*, 'the god's house').

King lists

In a royal mortuary temple, offerings of food were made to the deceased ruler. The accompanying rituals included prayers that it was believed would allow the king's *ka* or spirit to be nourished by the food. Endowments of land to the temple enabled these rituals to continue for generations after the death of the king to whom it was dedicated.

Some cenotaph temples, including those of the Nineteenth-Dynasty kings Ramesses II and Seti I at Abydos, contained kinglists recording almost all the rulers of Egypt, as well as shrines to various deities. After an offering of food had been made to a deity or the king and he was judged to have finished with it, it would be placed on an altar set before the kinglist so that it could also nourish all the previous kings. Once they were deemed to have been satisfied by the offering, it would be removed and given to the priests serving in the temple.

Tending the god

The most important temple rites were concerned with the washing and feeding of the god in the form of his statue. Every morning at dawn, the clay seal on the shrine was broken, and the door opened. Two purification rituals were performed before the god: incense was burnt and a libation of water was poured. He was believed to need a good breakfast, so food was brought to him as

▲ *Reliefs on the walls of Hatshepsut's mortuary temple at Deir el-Bahri show incense and other exotic goods being imported by boat from Punt. 18th Dynasty.*

an offering. The ancient Egyptians would certainly have agreed with the saying that cleanliness is next to godliness. The next stage of the proceedings was to remove the god so that his shrine could be cleaned. The

► *The two cartouches above Ramesses III's incense burner frame his throne name ('He of the Sedge and the Bee') and birth name ('son of Re'). Amunherkhopeshef's Tomb.*

statue was then undressed, cleansed with incense and water, re-dressed in clean linen, and adorned with jewellery, before being returned to his shrine. The rituals were accompanied by chanting and singing. Similar but less elaborate rituals were carried out at midday and in the evening. The rites were depicted on temple walls in the hope that even if the priesthood failed to perform them, the service would be guaranteed for eternity.

The god's shrine

The Greek word *naos* is generally used to refer to the shrine of the god. It was a rectangular box carved from a single block of wood or stone (often basalt or granite), with wooden doors. If the god needed to leave his *naos* to travel to a particular ceremony or festival, he would be carried on the shoulders of priests in a divine boat (a model of a real Nile vessel). If he needed to

travel, his barque was placed on an actual boat. Amun, for example, crossed the river at Thebes to the west bank for the Valley Festival, and Hathor travelled from her temple at Dendera to that of Horus at Edfu for the Feast of the Beautiful Meeting. Very often these barques had an *aegis* (a broad necklace surmounted with

the head of the deity in question) attached to the prow and stern. The barque of Amun, for example, was adorned with the head of a ram at each end. At the temple of Edfu the sacred barque stood on a plinth in front of the *naos*, while at the temples of Luxor and Karnak the gods had their own barque shrines.

► *Pediu-Imenet is depicted in his Book of the Dead making an offering of incense to Osiris. The fine quality of the dead man's linen clothing is indicated by its transparency. 21st–22nd Dynasty.*

Incense and water

Rites of purification would have been among the most important of the temple rituals. These included the burning of incense and the pouring of libations of water to the gods. The ancient Egyptians burnt a variety of aromatic substances, made from herbs, spices and resins, which were particularly highly prized because they had to be imported. The incenses were brought from the Mediterranean, and also from an east African land which the Egyptians called Punt (thought to be either modern day Eritrea or Somalia). Reliefs on the walls of Hatshepsut's mortuary temple at Deir el-Bahri show balls of a sweet-scented gum resin being brought by boat from Punt to Egypt. The trees from which this resin was tapped were called *antyw*-trees, which is often translated as 'myrrh'. The most common word for incense in general was *senetjer*, which is translated as 'to make divine', emphasizing its importance in religious ritual.

▶ *The animal's legs were usually extended to fit neatly alongside the body which was stretched, treated with resin and wrapped in natron-soaked linen bandages.*

◀ *A series of vaulted mudbrick cat cemeteries has been excavated at the site of Tell Basta (Bubastis), the cult centre of the goddess Bastet. Late Period.*

Pure water was also considered sacred by the ancient Egyptians, explaining the importance of the sacred lake within the temple complex (see *Temple Architecture*). The most common type of lake was called *she netjeri* ('divine pool'). It was a rectangular, stone-lined reservoir filled by groundwater, and examples have been found at temples such as Karnak, Dendera, and Medinet Habu. The remains of ablution tanks have also been discovered in temple confines, such as in the first court (now ruined) at Abydos; and near to chapels, such as the T-shaped pools close to the chapels in the workmen's village at Tell el-Amarna. Water drawn from the lake was used in the temple both for purification and as offering.

▶ *Not only might a dead animal be intricately mummified, but it might also be placed in a plastered and painted wooden coffin imitating the shape of the animal.*

Everlasting offerings

The ancient Egyptian word for 'offering', *hetep* was also their word for 'satisfaction'. The idea was that the gods and spirits of the dead were satisfied by the offerings of food and drink (and other things such as linen) that would be made to them.

The hieroglyphic sign for an offering, and an altar, was a mat (the forerunner to the more sophisticated offering table of stone) with a loaf of bread placed on it. In addition to the actual offerings that would have been placed on these tables, representations of them were carved on the stone surface – these were seen as magical substitutes for the real thing, thereby ensuring an eternal supply of symbolic sustenance for the gods.

The offerings that were depicted on the altar tables include jars of water, beer, wine and milk, trussed ducks and loaves of bread. Grooves that had been cut into the surface of the offering tables were intended to receive the libations that were poured from ceremonial vases. The most highly prized offerings made in the temples and tomb chapels consisted of the meat of oxen, the choice cut being the foreleg. It is clear that the animal itself was not sacrificed in the temple before the god, but was butchered in the temple butchery, and then the choice piece of meat was offered to the god (or the deceased person). The ritual significance of the ox's foreleg is emphasized by the fact that the oxon was also used as a symbol of royal and divine strength or power. ◆

Mummified animals

From the Late Period (c.747 BC) pilgrims to certain temples could purchase a mummified animal to offer to the gods. The animals were bred specially for this purpose, and were considered sacred. Having been dedicated to the particular deity, they were ritually buried at the cult centres, where they have been discovered literally in their millions. Subterranean chambers at Saqqara, for example, have yielded an estimated four million embalmed ibises. Today these animal mummies are scientifically studied, but as recently as the nineteenth century hundreds of tons of mummified cats were shipped from Egypt to the English port of Liverpool to be turned into fertilizer.

Temple Literature

We know that hymns, prayers, and incantations were sung, chanted or recited in the temples. These have been found inscribed on temple walls and on stone stelae erected in temple and burial complexes, as well as written on papyrus. It is most likely that they were composed and copied by the priesthood in a temple room such as the House of Life, where the most able scholars studied texts in all fields of knowledge, from funerary rituals to astronomy.

Ancient Egyptian prayers commonly took the form of a bargain made between the priest, deputizing for the king, and the god. The deal was that offerings were made to the deity in return for the granting of tangible favours or rewards, such as victory in battle or a long life.

Some ancient musical instruments have survived, together with representations of musicians. The title 'Temple Musician' is also found in texts, so hymns were presumably sung with an accompaniment, but no musical notation has survived from ancient Egypt – although we know the words we can have no idea of the kind of tunes to which they were set.

Hymns provide us with a great deal of information concerning the ancient Egyptian perception of the divine world – including the names, titles and epithets of gods and goddesses. In fact, some of the mythological details referred to in them add to our understanding of the myths themselves.

A huge number of funerary stelae have been found inscribed with a hymn to Osiris, the god of the dead and the Afterlife; many of the Nineteenth- and Twentieth-Dynasty royal tombs in the Valley of the Kings have inscribed on their walls a hymn to the sun god, known as the *Litany of Re*, which refers to the king as the son of the god.

▲ *The royal scribe Nebmertef writes on a papyrus roll under the auspices of the god Thoth, the patron deity of scribes, in the form of a baboon. New Kingdom.*

▼ *Granite statues of Senusret III from Deir el-Bahri display youthful, athletic bodies typical of royal statues, but the realistic portraiture of the aging faces is unusual.*

▶ *Offering bearers process with an array of offerings that include the foreleg of a ceremonially slaughtered ox, fish, and the spoils of desert hunting. 18th Dynasty.*

The Abusir Papyri

Of the more secular temple documents that have survived, perhaps the most informative are those known as the Abusir Papyri. These were the administrative documents of the mortuary cult of the Fifth-Dynasty king Neferirkare (c.2475–c.2455 BC), so they would have formed part of an archive housed in the funerary temple complex associated with this ruler's pyramid at Abusir, which was part of the necropolis of Memphis. The documents provide many details of the daily routine and organization of a mortuary temple, which would have continued for generations after the death of the king.

The numerous fragments that have been discovered feature lists of temple staff and their duties, including guard duties, corresponding to the regular daily and monthly rituals as well as the special arrangements for festivals. They outline the general organization of the temple workforce, and stipulate the offerings to be made. They also include inventories of the temple furnishings and cult objects, such as knives, vessels, boxes and jewellery, as well as records of the daily income and expenditure of the temple – accounts of all produce and materials arriving at the temple, their use or storage, and any financial transactions made. They record the quantity and variety of goods that poured into the temple from the royal estates and other institutions. There are also records of temple inspections, including checking for any damage to the stonework. ◆

Hymns to the king

A particularly splendid example of a collection of hymns is the cycle of six hymns sung in honour of the Twelfth-Dynasty king Senusret III (c.1874–c.1855 BC). All six hymns were written on one side of a large sheet of papyrus measuring 114cm (45in) across, discovered at the town of Kahun, which was home to those who worked on the pyramid construction and for the mortuary cult of Senusret III at el-Lahun. They were probably composed to be sung on the occasion of a royal visit, or perhaps they formed part of the service of the cult at the pyramid complex. The ruler was eulogized in poetic and – as one might expect – exaggerated, terms. He was identified with the supreme solar deity, Re:

He is Re, little are a thousand other men!

and with the ferocious lioness goddess Sekhmet:

He is Sekhmet to foes who tread on his frontier!

Akhenaten's Religious Revolution

Akhenaten (c.1352–c.1336 BC) was the tenth ruler of the Eighteenth Dynasty. His wife was the beautiful Queen Nefertiti. Akhenaten's reign saw enormous innovation and change. He chose to alter the state religion and mode of worship, and changed the style and content of art and temple architecture to such an extreme that his actions and beliefs have been heralded as revolutionary (he was considered heretical by later rulers).

He began his reign as Amenhotep IV – with the same name as his father, which meant 'Amun is Satisfied', but five years later he had changed his name to Akhenaten ('Beneficence of the Aten'), had extended the name of his wife to Neferneferuaten ('Fair is the beauty of the Aten'), and had founded a new capital called Akhetaten ('Horizon of the Aten'). At the centre of all this innovation and upheaval was the Aten (a manifestation of the solar deity, represented as the sun's disc) which Akhenaten elevated to the status of sole god in an attempt to eliminate the traditional pantheon. The plethora of gods and goddesses, with all the myths, festivals and rituals associated with them, were set aside for the duration of one king's reign. Or were they?

◀ *Nefertiti kisses her daughter. The art of the Amarna Period is characterized by a more intimate portrayal of the royal family than is found at any other time in ancient Egypt. 18th Dynasty.*

Akhenaten's New City

When Akhenaten began his reign, the administrative capital was Memphis and the greatest religious centre was Thebes, which was the home town of the ruling family of the Eighteenth Dynasty. Thebes was also home to the largest and wealthiest temple complex and the most powerful priesthood in the country – that of Amun at Karnak. It had benefited enormously from royal favours, vast quantities of tithes and the booty of war, especially resulting from the military campaigns of Tuthmosis III (c.1479–c.1425 BC) in Syria-Palestine. Because its might had consequently become overwhelming, it was in the interest of the status of kingship for Akhenaten to remove power from the temple of Amun and its High Priest. He achieved this by elevating a deity named the Aten to a position of supremacy and excluding from the state religion all other deities, including (and perhaps especially) Amun (see *Akhenaten's New Religion*). He also founded a new religious centre of Egypt, which became his administrative capital and the site of his royal palace.

In the fifth year of his reign, Akhenaten founded his new capital at the border between Middle and Upper Egypt, on the east bank of the Nile, about 280km (175 miles) south of Cairo. His decision to move the capital was probably politically motivated, but the site he chose was a virgin one, which meant that it had no existing religious associations. It was a wide plain approximately 10km (6 miles) long and a maximum of 5km (3 miles) wide, with perfect natural boundaries: the river lay to the west and desert cliffs formed a semicircular bay to the north, east and south (almost descending into the river at each end). Akhenaten had boundary

▶ *The ancient city of Akhetaten once stood on this desert plain on the east bank of the Nile, sheltered by a bay of cliffs.*

◀ *This vignette at the top of one of the boundary stelae at Tell el-Amarna illustrates that the Aten was worshipped in the open air in broad daylight, rather than within darkened temple sanctuaries as was the custom with other cults.*

▶ *The remains of this house in the central city exemplify the perennial problem of windswept sand in Egypt.*

stelae erected to designate the site of his city-to-be. The inscriptions on them dedicated all the buildings and their inhabitants to the Aten.

A large city, including housing of all sizes, palaces, temples, workshops, factories, bakeries and administrative buildings, was swiftly erected on the site. Many of the structures were enormous, elaborate and highly decorated, but because of the speed with which they had to be built, they were largely of mudbrick, and consequently very little has survived. The buildings were decorated using sunk relief, rather than the favoured, but incredibly time-consuming, raised relief.

The horizon of the Aten

Akhenaten called this city, with its columned halls, lush gardens, painted pavements and open courts, Akhetaten, 'The Horizon of the Aten'. Today the site is known as Tell el-Amarna, a name fabricated by nineteenth-century European visitors to the area. It is a misnomer because the site is not on a *tell* (Arabic for 'mound') created by successive building, as is usually the case with ancient settlement sites. Not only was Akhetaten built on virgin soil, but when the city was abandoned not long after Akhenaten's death it was never again built on or inhabited. The name Tell el-Amarna was probably derived from the names of the modern village of et-Till (and possibly the village of el-Amariya), and an Arab tribe called the Beni Amran, which had

settled and given its name to the district and a town on the west bank that belonged to it. The name Amarna has come to be used to refer to this particular period of Egyptian history.

Estimates of the ancient city's population range between 20,000 and 50,000, but it is usually said to have been about 30,000. (It has been worked out that the agricultural land at the city's disposal could have supported a population of 45,000.) As well as the city itself, archaeology at the site has revealed a walled village in the desert, about 1.2km (³/₄ mile) east of the main city, today known as the Workmen's Village. Further east still there is a collection of drystone housing, as yet unexcavated, called the Stone Village.

Akhenaten was not to know that his new capital would be abandoned after his death, and so provisions were made for the burial of the royal family and high officials in the desert cliffs surrounding the city. Two sets of rock-cut tombs, one to the north and one to the south, have been discovered, as has the royal tomb complex a short distance to the east of the desert cliffs. Most of the tombs were never finished. ◆

Excavating the site

Archaeologists have been working at the site of Tell el-Amarna pretty much systematically and continuously for the last century. The first significant excavations of the city were carried out by Sir William Matthew Flinders Petrie during the 1891/92 season. In 1911 a German team went on to gain the concession at the site for four seasons, under the direction of Ludwig Borchardt. The concession was regained by the British Egypt Exploration Society in 1921, and its excavations continued until 1936 (under the direction of Eric Peet, Leonard Woolley, Henri Frankfort and, lastly, John Pendlebury). In the 1960s the Egyptian Antiquities Organization carried out some work. But the most accurate and scientific archaeological excavation of the site and analysis of the material has been carried out on behalf of the Egypt Exploration Society by Barry Kemp and his colleagues since 1977.

Akhenaten's New Religion

▲ *In exchange for the offerings made by the royal family, the hands at the ends of the Aten's rays hold* ankhs *to the noses of the king and queen on this sculpted block from the Great Palace at Tell el-Amarna.*

▲ *High officials were usually represented as proud and upright in Egyptian art, but during the Amarna Period they were shown bowing before the king. 18th Dynasty. Tomb of Ramose, Thebes.*

T he imagery and inscriptions of Akhenaten's reign reveal that he elevated one god to the unique position of sole deity, and instituted measures to eliminate all other deities. The emphasis on the importance of the sun god was not new, but his sole worship was unprecedented. Later in his reign, Akhenaten sent agents throughout Egypt to destroy the cult statues of other deities and excise their names (even that of Amun in his father's cartouche). By dispensing with the representations of a multitude of deities as weird and wonderful combinations of humans and animals, and with the myths associated with them, Akhenaten seems to have been attempting the creation of a purer and simpler religious doctrine, void of mysticism.

There was nothing innovative about the expression of devotion to the sun god, but Akhenaten took the age-old solar worship to an extreme never before experienced in Egypt. The sun, in the divine personification of Re, had been associated with kingship from at least as early as the Fourth Dynasty (c.2500 BC), when the king first took the epithet 'Son of Re'.

The Aten

Akhenaten chose to worship the simplest manifestation of the sun – the disc of the sun itself – the Aten. The Aten was not new; in fact, one of the best-known pieces of Egyptian literature, the Twelfth-Dynasty *Tale of Sinuhe* (c.1900 BC), tells us that when Amenemhat I died he ascended to join the Aten in the heavens. The popularity of the Aten had been growing since the beginning of the New Kingdom: Tuthmosis I (c.1504–c.1492 BC), for example, had taken the title, 'Horus-Re who comes from the Aten', and Amenhotep III (c.1390–c.1352 BC) had named his royal boat 'Glorious is the Aten'. There was certainly a temple to the Aten at Karnak by the reign of Amenhotep III.

▲ *This stela from Tell el-Amarna clearly shows the informality of royal portraiture. Akhenaten gives an earring to his daughter Meritaten, while two princesses sit on Nefertiti's lap. 18th Dynasty.*

▶ *This colossal sandstone statue of Akhenaten from the site of the Gempaaten temple at Karnak shows the unorthodox representation of the king (a style that was more exaggerated at the beginning of his reign). 18th Dynasty.*

The Aten had come to be represented as the solar deity Re-Horakhty – a hawk-headed man with a sun disc on his head – but early in his reign, Akhenaten put an end to this, and the Aten was to be represented purely as a sun disc. However, the disc did have some of the attributes of the deities that had been rejected. Its rays ended in hands, some of which held *ankhs* (the sign of life). Like the king, the disc wore a *uraeus* (a rearing cobra ready to spit venom at the king or god's enemies), had its names written in cartouches, and a pharaonic titulary. In fact it could be said that the focus of Akhenaten's new religion was really the royal family, whose divine status he stressed. In art, the Aten was depicted holding out *ankhs* only to the mouths and nostrils of immediate members of the royal family. It appears that only the royal family was believed to benefit from the life-giving powers of the sun, and only they might worship the sun directly. Families throughout the city of Akhetaten had household shrines, not with a stela or figurine depicting one of the traditional deities, or one of their ancestors, as we might expect, but a stela or figure of the king and/or his wife and children. They, in turn, were shown interacting with the Aten. The focus of these shrine images was quite clearly the royal family, and there is no expression of an individual's direct relationship with the god.

Bizarre bodies

Akhenaten claimed to 'live on *maat*' ('truth', 'order', 'justice') as previously only the gods had been said to. He also chose to have himself (and members of his family) depicted in a decidedly unconventional and distinctive character – with full lips, snake eyes, a long neck, pendulous breasts, a paunch, spindly limbs and swollen hips, buttocks and thighs – a far cry from the strong athletic bodies of the traditional depictions of kings. We do not know why Akhenaten chose to have himself represented in this way, but it may have been an attempt to conjure up a divine persona for himself.

His reign also saw the construction of temples of a new design. We must forget the characteristic style of Egyptian temples – the dark inner sanctuary and cult statue – and must imagine instead large open courts with innumerable altars, so that the Aten was very much worshipped in the open air. The shadowy mystery of the traditional temple had gone. Temples dedicated to the traditional deities were closed down throughout Egypt, and as the temple would have been the centre of the local economy it can be assumed that this heavy-handed policy would have resulted in a certain amount of social unrest and hardship.

▲ The two princesses sitting at the feet of their mother Nefertiti in this wall painting display the extended skull characteristic of Amarna-period portraiture.

King of the Afterlife

Because Akhenaten had done away with the traditional funerary deities, and the myths associated with them, the concept of the Afterlife had to be cast aside (at least at an official level). With Osiris abandoned, Akhenaten claimed to be the ruler not only of the living, but also of the dead. The funerary rites previously deemed necessary for entrance into the Afterlife no longer applied, and the rock-cut desert tombs at Amarna for the administrative elite were very differently decorated to those at Thebes. The private individual was no longer the protagonist in his own tomb. There were no more scenes of funerary rituals, or the Afterlife, or of daily life in the Nile Valley, or of the tomb owner in the presence of the deities. Now Akhenaten and his family were the centre of attention in every tomb, in scenes illustrating their daily activities, and the tomb owner himself was depicted tiny and humble before the king.

Realistically there is no way that Akhenaten could have obliterated the religious beliefs and superstitions of his people. Despite the dogma issued by the government, and the public displays of devotion to the royal family and acknowledgement of the supremacy of the Aten, in private the people of Egypt must have continued to worship the traditional deities, particularly the household gods and goddesses to whom they felt able to relate directly. In fact many amulets, stelae, rings, pendants and other objects representing the traditional deities of Egypt have been found at Tell el-Amarna dating from this period. How could a pregnant woman forget Taweret, for example, when this goddess might be able to help her through a difficult birth? ◆

Thutmose the sculptor

The prize possession of the Egyptian museum collection in Berlin is a painted limestone bust of Queen Nefertiti wearing a tall blue crown (48cm [19in] high), which was found at Akhetaten. It is the work of a sculptor called Thutmose and was found in his studio, close to his house in a part of the south suburb of the city where other sculptors lived and had their workshops.

The Restoration of Traditional Religion

There is archaeological evidence for the increasing importance of the Aten, and interesting changes in artistic style, during the reign of Akhenaten's predecessor Amenhotep III (c.1390– c.1352 BC) – whether or not the two shared a co-regency is still disputed. But it is Akhenaten (c.1352–1336 BC) who was – and still is – regarded as the innovator, if not revolutionary. Soon after his death he was branded a heretic and his ideas and style were quashed.

On Akhenaten's death, he was succeeded by an ephemeral ruler named Smenkhkare (c.1338–c.1336 BC) who, it has been argued, might actually have been Nefertiti, and who was probably sole ruler for only a few months. Smenkhkare's successor probably grew up at Akhetaten, and began his life as Tutankhaten ('Living Image of the Aten'). He was, of course, Tutankhamun (c.1336–c.1327 BC), whose name means

'Living Image of Amun'. He must have changed his name to distance himself from the Atenist cult and the heretical practices of Akhenaten, who was quite possibly his father (his mother being a minor wife, Kiya). Tutankhamun had married one of Akhenaten's daughters by Nefertiti, Ankhsenpaaten, who in turn changed her name to Ankhsenamun.

Tutankhamun's reign witnessed the reinstallation of the traditional religion of Egypt. Akhetaten was abandoned and Memphis once again became the administrative capital of Egypt, with Thebes as the main religious centre. Tutankhamun issued a decree regarding the return to polytheism; his reforms have been found inscribed on a stela at Karnak temple. This is known as the Restoration Stela and is now in the Cairo Museum.

It was not until the reign of Horemheb (c.1323–c.1295 BC), who had been the Great

◄ *Tutankhamun and his wife are depicted seated beneath the rays of the Aten on the back of this gold-plated and inlaid wooden throne. 18th Dynasty.*

▲ *Gold necklaces were bestowed as rewards by the king on his loyal entourage. Here Horemheb receives such a gift in his post as Tutankhamun's Commander of the Army and King's Deputy.*

Commander of the army under Akhenaten but became the last ruler of the Eighteenth Dynasty, that Egypt experienced a violent backlash to the Amarna Period. The eradication of Akhetaten began, and the cartouches and images of Akhenaten and Nefertiti were defaced. The aim was to remove all traces of the cult of the Aten, to the extent that Akhenaten's name was missed out of later New Kingdom lists of kings (together with those of Smenkhkare, and even Tutankhamun and Ay, his successor). When Akhenaten's name did come up, he was referred to as 'the heretic' or 'the rebel').

Ironically, the demolished stone blocks, or *talata* (from the Arabic 'three hand-breadths', describing their dimensions) from Akhenaten's temples did survive. They were used as rubble infill in the walls and pylons of later temples dedicated to traditional deities, such as Horemheb's ninth and tenth pylons at the temple of Amun at Karnak. ◆

Index

Acknowledgements

AKG Photographic p8–9 (British Museum, London), p15 bottom (Aegyptisches Museum, Berlin), p35 (Aegyptisches Museum, Berlin), p38 top, p45 bottom, p46, p49 right (Louvre, Paris), p56 top and bottom, p65 top, p66, p67 Kunsthistorisches Museum, p80, p86 bottom (Rijksmuseum van Oudheden), p94–95, p108 right, p112, p115 (Roemer-Pelizaeus Museum, Hildesheim), p122 left (Egyptian Museum, Cairo)

A M Dodson p26 right, p78 top (Museum of Metropolitan Art, New York)

The Ancient Art & Architecture Collection p16, p18 bottom, p19, p31 left, p34 right, p39, p52 bottom, p74 top, p79, p81 left, p82, p83 bottom, p84, p96 top and bottom, p103, p104, p105 bottom, p106 bottom, p110 left, p113 top and bottom, p120 top, p123 right

The Ancient Egypt Picture Library p18 top, p26 left (British Museum, London), p38 bottom (British Museum, London), p45 top, p49 left, p54 bottom, p55 (Fitzwilliam Museum, University of Cambridge), p60 (Egyptian Museum, Cairo), p63 top (Egyptian Museum, Cairo), p67 top, p70 left (Louvre, Paris), p74 bottom (Egyptian Museum, Cairo), p77 (Egyptian Museum, Cairo), p83 top, (British Museum, London), p87 top (British Museum, London), p88 bottom (Louvre, Paris), p89 top and bottom, p97 bottom, p99 top, p100, p102 bottom, p109 top, p114 right (British Museum, London), p116 bottom (British Museum, London), p125 top, p90 bottom, p91, p92

The Art Archive p15 top (British Museum, London), p20 top, p29 bottom (Louvre, Paris), p33 Egyptian Museum, Cairo), p36 top (British Museum, London), p44 bottom, p51 top left (Egyptian Museum, Cairo), p54 top (Egyptian Museum, Turin), p57,

p64 (Egyptian Museum, Cairo), p69 (British Museum, London), p75, top (Egyptian Museum, Cairo), p81 right (Louvre, Paris), p86 bottom (Egyptian Museum, Cairo), p88 top (British Museum, London), p107, p110 right (Egyptian Museum, Cairo), p114 left (Louvre, Paris)

The Bridgeman Art Library p2 (British Museum, London), p10 bottom (Fitzwilliam Museum, Cambridge), p11 (Louvre, Paris), p17 top (British Museum, London, p17 bottom (Louvre, Paris), p23 top (Louvre, Paris), p23 bottom (British Museum, London), p24 (Louvre, Paris), p25 right (Bonhams, London), p28 (Ashmolean Museum, Oxford), p29 top (British Museum, London), p34 left (British Museum, London), p36 bottom (Ashmolean Museum, Oxford), p37 right (Louvre, Paris), p37 left (Ashmolean Museum, Oxford), p40–41, p42 (Louvre, Paris), p51 bottom (Fitzwilliam Museum, University of Cambridge), p72 (Louvre, Paris), p86 top (Egyptian Museum, Turin), p90 top (Louvre, Paris), p102 top, p108 left (British Museum, London), p116 top (Louvre), p117 (Louvre, Paris), p122 right, p124 (Ashmolean Museum, Oxford)

The Hutchinson Library p47 top

Lucia Gahlin p47 bottom, p62, p78 bottom, p97 top, p105 top, p106 top, p120 bottom, p121

Michael Holford p68 left, p73 top (British Museum, London)

Peter Clayton p109 bottom

Robert Harding p52 top, p53 top and bottom (both Egyptian Museum, Cairo), p71, p125 left

Sylvia Cordaiy Photo Library p43 top (Guy Marks), p44 top, p48 (Johnathan Smith), p98 top

Travel Ink p98 bottom

Werner Forman Archive
p10 top, p12 (Dr E Strouhal), p13 bottom left and right, p14 (Louvre, Paris), p20 bottom (E Strouhal), p21, p22 (Egyptian Museum, Cairo), p25 left (private collection), p27 (Egyptian Museum, Cairo), p30 (British Museum, London), p31 right (Egyptian Museum, Cairo), p32 left (Egyptian Museum, Cairo), p32 right (E Strouhal), p50 (Cheops Barque Museum), p51 top right, p58–59, p61 (Manchester Museum), p63 (Metropolitan Museum of Art, New York), p65 bottom (Graeco-Roman Museum, Alexandria), p68 right (Rijksmuseum van Oudeheden, Leiden), p70 right (Aegyptisches Museum, Berlin), p73 bottom (Fitzwilliam Museum, University of Cambridge), p75 (Sold at Christie's, London), p76 (British Museum, London), p85, p93, (Egyptian Museum, Cairo), p101 top and bottom, p111 (Louvre, Paris), p118–119 (Brooklyn Museum, New York), p123 left (Egyptian Museum, Cairo)